9596-269

STRESS
MANAGEMENT

GENERAL EDITORS

Dale C. Garell, M.D.
Medical Director, California Children Services, Department of Health
    Services, County of Los Angeles
Associate Dean for Curriculum
Clinical Professor, Department of Pediatrics & Family Medicine,
    University of Southern California School of Medicine
Former President, Society for Adolescent Medicine

Solomon H. Snyder, M.D.
Distinguished Service Professor of Neuroscience, Pharmacology, and
    Psychiatry, Johns Hopkins University School of Medicine
Former president, Society of Neuroscience
Albert Lasker Award in Medical Research, 1978

CONSULTING EDITORS

Robert W. Blum, M.D., Ph.D.
Associate Professor, School of Public Health and Department of
    Pediatrics
Director, Adolescent Health Program, University of Minnesota
Consultant, World Health Organization

Charles E. Irwin, Jr., M.D.
Associate Professor of Pediatrics; Director, Division of Adolescent
    Medicine, University of California, San Francisco

Lloyd J. Kolbe, Ph.D.
Chief, Office of School Health & Special Projects, Center for Health
    Promotion & Education, Centers for Disease Control
President, American School Health Association

Jordan J. Popkin
Director, Division of Federal Employee Occupational Health, U.S. Public
    Health Service Region I

Joseph L. Rauh, M.D.
Professor of Pediatrics and Medicine, Adolescent Medicine, Children's
    Hospital Medical Center, Cincinnati
Former president, Society for Adolescent Medicine

THE ENCYCLOPEDIA OF

H E A L T H

PSYCHOLOGICAL DISORDERS
AND THEIR TREATMENT

Solomon H. Snyder, M.D. · General Editor

STRESS MANAGEMENT

James S. Gordon, M.D.

Introduction by C. Everett Koop, M.D., Sc.D.
former Surgeon General, U.S. Public Health Service

CHELSEA HOUSE PUBLISHERS
New York · Philadelphia

ON THE COVER Detail of a damned soul, from *The Last Judgement* by Michelangelo.

Chelsea House Publishers
EDITOR-IN-CHIEF Nancy Toff
EXECUTIVE EDITOR Remmel T. Nunn
MANAGING EDITOR Karyn Gullen Browne
COPY CHIEF Juliann Barbato
PICTURE EDITOR Adrian G. Allen
ART DIRECTOR Maria Epes
MANUFACTURING MANAGER Gerald Levine

The Encyclopedia of Health
SENIOR EDITOR Paula Edelson

Staff for STRESS MANAGEMENT
ASSOCIATE EDITOR Will Broaddus
COPY EDITOR Brian Sookram
DEPUTY COPY CHIEF Mark Rifkin
EDITORIAL ASSISTANT Leigh Hope Wood
PICTURE RESEARCHER Georganne Backman
ASSISTANT ART DIRECTOR Loraine Machlin
SENIOR DESIGNER Marjorie Zaum
DESIGN ASSISTANT Debora Smith
PRODUCTION MANAGER Joseph Romano
PRODUCTION COORDINATOR Marie Claire Cebrián

5 7 9 8 6 4

Library of Congress Cataloging-in-Publication Data

Gordon, James S. (James Samuel)
  Stress management / James S. Gordon.
    p. cm.—(The Encylopedia of health)
  Includes bibliographical references.
  Summary: Discusses various aspects of stress management, including
the nature and biology of stress, ecological and psychosocial
aspects, techniques for stress reduction, and stress management
programs.
  ISBN 0-7910-0042-7
      0-7910-0516-X (pbk.)
  1. Stress management—Juvenile literature. [1. Stress
management.] I. Title. II. Series.   89-25293
RA785.G67 1990   CIP
155.9′042—dc20   AC

CONTENTS

The goal of the ENCYCLOPEDIA OF HEALTH *is to provide general information in the ever-changing areas of physiology, psychology, and related medical issues. The titles in this series are not intended to take the place of the professional advice of a physician or other health care professional.*

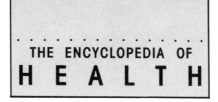

THE ENCYCLOPEDIA OF
H E A L T H

PREVENTION AND EDUCATION: THE KEYS TO GOOD HEALTH

C. Everett Koop, M.D., Sc.D.
former Surgeon General,
U.S. Public Health Service

The issue of health education has received particular attention in recent years because of the presence of AIDS in the news. But our response to this particular tragedy points up a number of broader issues that doctors, public health officials, educators, and the public face. In particular, it points up the necessity for sound health education for citizens of all ages.

Over the past 25 years this country has been able to bring about dramatic declines in the death rates for heart disease, stroke, accidents, and, for people under the age of 45, cancer. Today, Americans generally eat better and take better care of themselves than ever before. Thus, with the help of modern science and technology, they have a better chance of surviving serious—even catastrophic— illnesses. That's the good news.

But, like every phonograph record, there's a flip side, and one with special significance for young adults. According to a report issued in 1979 by Dr. Julius Richmond, my predecessor as Surgeon General, Americans aged 15 to 24 had a higher death rate in 1979 than they did 20 years earlier. The causes: violent death and injury, alcohol and drug abuse, unwanted pregnancies, and sexually transmitted diseases. Adolescents are particularly vulnerable because they are beginning to explore their own sexuality and perhaps to experiment with drugs. The need for educating young people is critical, and the price of neglect is high.

Yet even for the population as a whole, our health is still far from what it could be. Why? A 1974 Canadian government report attributed all death and disease to four broad elements: inadequacies in

7

the health care system, behavioral factors or unhealthy life-styles, environmental hazards, and human biological factors.

To be sure, there are diseases that are still beyond the control of even our advanced medical knowledge and techniques. And despite yearnings that are as old as the human race itself, there is no "fountain of youth" to ward off aging and death. Still, there is a solution to many of the problems that undermine sound health. In a word, that solution is prevention. Prevention, which includes health promotion and education, saves lives, improves the quality of life, and, in the long run, saves money.

In the United States, organized public health activities and preventive medicine have a long history. Important milestones include the improvement of sanitary procedures and the development of pasteurized milk in the late 19th century, and the introduction in the mid-20th century of effective vaccines against polio, measles, German measles, mumps, and other once-rampant diseases. Internationally, organized public health efforts began on a wide-scale basis with the International Sanitary Conference of 1851, to which 12 nations sent representatives. The World Health Organization, founded in 1948, continues these efforts under the aegis of the United Nations, with particular emphasis on combatting communicable diseases and the training of health care workers.

Despite these accomplishments, much remains to be done in the field of prevention. For too long, we have had a medical care system that is science- and technology-based, focused, essentially, on illness and mortality. It is now patently obvious that both the social and the economic costs of such a system are becoming insupportable.

Implementing prevention—and its corollaries, health education and promotion—is the job of several groups of people.

First, the medical and scientific professions need to continue basic scientific research, and here we are making considerable progress. But increased concern with prevention will also have a decided impact on how primary care doctors practice medicine. With a shift to health-based rather than morbidity-based medicine, the role of the "new physician" will include a healthy dose of patient education.

Second, practitioners of the social and behavioral sciences—psychologists, economists, city planners—along with lawyers, business leaders, and government officials—must solve the practical and ethical dilemmas confronting us: poverty, crime, civil rights, literacy, education, employment, housing, sanitation, environmental protection, health care delivery systems, and so forth. All of these issues affect public health.

Third is the public at large. We'll consider that very important group in a moment.

Fourth, and the linchpin in this effort, is the public health profession—doctors, epidemiologists, teachers—who must harness the professional expertise of the first two groups and the common sense and cooperation of the third, the public. They must define the problems statistically and qualitatively and then help us set priorities for finding the solutions.

To a very large extent, improving those statistics is the responsibility of every individual. So let's consider more specifically what the role of the individual should be and why health education is so important to that role. First, and most obviously, individuals can protect themselves from illness and injury and thus minimize their need for professional medical care. They can eat nutritious food, get adequate exercise, avoid tobacco, alcohol, and drugs, and take prudent steps to avoid accidents. The proverbial "apple a day keeps the doctor away" is not so far from the truth, after all.

Second, individuals should actively participate in their own medical care. They should schedule regular medical and dental checkups. Should they develop an illness or injury, they should know when to treat themselves and when to seek professional help. To gain the maximum benefit from any medical treatment that they do require, individuals must become partners in that treatment. For instance, they should understand the effects and side effects of medications. I counsel young physicians that there is no such thing as too much information when talking with patients. But the corollary is the patient must know enough about the nuts and bolts of the healing process to understand what the doctor is telling him. That is at least partially the patient's responsibility.

Education is equally necessary for us to understand the ethical and public policy issues in health care today. Sometimes individuals will encounter these issues in making decisions about their own treatment or that of family members. Other citizens may encounter them as jurors in medical malpractice cases. But we all become involved, indirectly, when we elect our public officials, from school board members to the president. Should surrogate parenting be legal? To what extent is drug testing desirable, legal, or necessary? Should there be public funding for family planning, hospitals, various types of medical research, and medical care for the indigent? How should we allocate scant technological resources, such as kidney dialysis and organ transplants? What is the proper role of government in protecting the rights of patients?

What are the broad goals of public health in the United States today? In 1980, the Public Health Service issued a report aptly entitled *Promoting Health—Preventing Disease: Objectives for the Nation*. This report expressed its goals in terms of mortality and in

9

terms of intermediate goals in education and health improvement. It identified 15 major concerns: controlling high blood pressure; improving family planning; improving pregnancy care and infant health; increasing the rate of immunization; controlling sexually transmitted diseases; controlling the presence of toxic agents and radiation in the environment; improving occupational safety and health; preventing accidents; promoting water fluoridation and dental health; controlling infectious diseases; decreasing smoking; decreasing alcohol and drug abuse; improving nutrition; promoting physical fitness and exercise; and controlling stress and violent behavior.

For healthy adolescents and young adults (ages 15 to 24), the specific goal was a 20% reduction in deaths, with a special focus on motor vehicle injuries and alcohol and drug abuse. For adults (ages 25 to 64), the aim was 25% fewer deaths, with a concentration on heart attacks, strokes, and cancers.

Smoking is perhaps the best example of how individual behavior can have a direct impact on health. Today cigarette smoking is recognized as the most important single preventable cause of death in our society. It is responsible for more cancers and more cancer deaths than any other known agent; is a prime risk factor for heart and blood vessel disease, chronic bronchitis, and emphysema; and is a frequent cause of complications in pregnancies and of babies born prematurely, underweight, or with potentially fatal respiratory and cardiovascular problems.

Since the release of the Surgeon General's first report on smoking in 1964, the proportion of adult smokers has declined substantially, from 43% in 1965 to 30.5% in 1985. Since 1965, 37 million people have quit smoking. Although there is still much work to be done if we are to become a "smoke-free society," it is heartening to note that public health and public education efforts—such as warnings on cigarette packages and bans on broadcast advertising—have already had significant effects.

In 1835, Alexis de Tocqueville, a French visitor to America, wrote, "In America the passion for physical well-being is general." Today, as then, health and fitness are front-page items. But with the greater scientific and technological resources now available to us, we are in a far stronger position to make good health care available to everyone. And with the greater technological threats to us as we approach the 21st century, the need to do so is more urgent than ever before. Comprehensive information about basic biology, preventive medicine, medical and surgical treatments, and related ethical and public policy issues can help you arm yourself with the knowledge you need to be healthy throughout your life.

FOREWORD

Solomon H. Snyder, M.D.

Mental disorders represent the number one health problem for the United States and probably for the entire human population. Some studies estimate that approximately one-third of all Americans suffer from some sort of emotional disturbance. Depression of varying severity will affect as many as 20 percent of all of us at one time or another in our lives. Severe anxiety is even more common.

Adolescence is a time of particular susceptibility to emotional problems. Teenagers are undergoing significant changes in their brain as well as their physical structure. The hormones that alter the organs of reproduction during puberty also influence the way we think and feel. At a purely psychological level, adolescents must cope with major upheavals in their lives. After years of not noticing the opposite sex, they find themselves romantically attracted but must painfully learn the skills of social interchange both for superficial, flirtatious relationships and for genuine intimacy. Teenagers must develop new ways of relating to their parents. Adolescents strive for independence. Yet, our society is structured in such a way that teenagers must remain dependent on their parents for many more years. During adolescence, young men and women examine their own intellectual bents and begin to plan the type of higher education and vocation they believe they will find most fulfilling.

Because of all these challenges, teenagers are more emotionally volatile than adults. Passages from extreme exuberance to dejection are common. The emotional distress of completely normal adolescence can be so severe that the same disability in an adult would be labeled as major mental illness. Although most teenagers somehow muddle through and emerge unscathed, a number of problems are more frequent among adolescents than among adults. Many psychological aberrations reflect severe disturbances, although these are sometimes not regarded as "psychiatric." Eating disorders, to which young adults are especially vulnerable, are an example. An extremely large number of teenagers diet to great excess even though they are not overweight. Many of them suffer from a specific disturbance referred to as anorexia nervosa, a form of self-starvation that is just as real a disorder as diabetes. The same is true for those who eat compulsively and then sometimes force themselves to vomit. They may be afflicted with bulimia.

Depression is also surprisingly frequent among adolescents, although its symptoms may be less obvious in young people than they are in adults. And, because suicide occurs most frequently in those suffering from depression, we must be on the lookout for subtle hints of despondency in those close to us. This is especially urgent because teenage suicide is a rapidly worsening national problem.

The volumes on Psychological Disorders and Their Treatment in the ENCYCLOPEDIA OF HEALTH cover the major areas of mental illness, from mild to severe. They also emphasize the means available for getting help. *Anxiety and Phobias, Depression*, and *Schizophrenia* deal specifically with these forms of mental disturbance. *Child Abuse* and *Delinquency and Criminal Behavior* explore abnormalities of behavior that may stem from environmental and social influences as much as from biological or psychological illness. *Personality Disorders* and *Compulsive Behavior* explain how people develop disturbances of their overall personality. *Learning Disabilities* investigates disturbances of the mind that may reflect neurological derangements as much as psychological abnormalities. *Mental Retardation* explains the various causes of this many-sided handicap, including the genetic component, complications during pregnancy, and traumas during birth. *Suicide* discusses the epidemiology of this tragic phenomenon and outlines the assistance available to those who are at risk. *Stress Management* locates the sources of stress in contemporary society and considers formal strategies for coping with it. Finally, *Diagnosing and Treating Mental Illness* explains to the reader how professionals sift through various signs and symptoms to define the exact nature of the various mental disorders and fully describes the most effective means of alleviating them.

Fortunately, when it comes to psychological disorders, knowing the facts is a giant step toward solving the problems.

CHAPTER 1

WHAT IS STRESS?

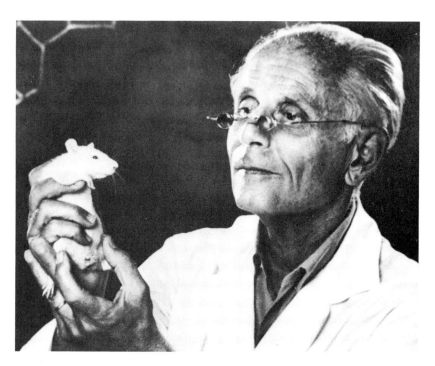

Hans Selye

The concept of stress has become a familiar one, describing the variety of physical, psychological, and social problems that can cause illness and discomfort in varying degrees. These problems include the wars, pollution, poverty, noise, crime, and overcrowding that are an increasing part of the modern world. Simple everyday irritations such as anxiety or nervousness are often classified as stress. Physicians sometimes tell their patients that their illnesses are "stress related." One may wonder if this or that activity, relationship, or way of thinking or feeling increases or decreases stress levels. And, sooner or later, those who do suffer from it must ask themselves, or someone else, if there is anything they can do to manage their level of stress and the physical or emotional problems it seems to produce. The concept of stress was not a subject people discussed or were even familiar with until 1936. That was the year the Canadian physician and physiologist Hans Selye first described it in his book *The Stress of Life*, in which he put forward the following definition: "Stress is the state manifested by a specific syndrome which consists of all the nonspecifically induced changes within a biological system." Later, he simplified the concept: "Stress," he declared, "is the nonspecific response of the body to any demand."

After he finished his medical training, Selye set out to see whether there was a biological basis to this "syndrome of just being sick," a consistent set of anatomical and physiological reactions that occurred when many different "noxious stimuli" were applied to the body. In a landmark series of experiments, he exposed laboratory rats to extreme heat and cold and to electrical shocks and injected them with a variety of poisons and irritations to their nervous system. Each of these stimuli produced specific local reactions that differed from one stimulus to the other, but all of them produced a series of reactions that were remarkably consistent from one stimulus to the next.

After performing laboratory examinations and autopsies on the rats, Selye noted the following consistent pattern of changes after exposure to many different kinds of stress:

1. Enlargement of the cortex or outer portion of the adrenal gland (which secretes adrenocortical hormones, which improve overall physiological functioning and reduce inflammation)

2. Shrinkage of the thymus, spleen, and lymph nodes (all of which produce cells that protect the body against invasion by outside forces such as bacteria)

3. Bleeding ulcers in the stomach and small intestine (resulting from the high level of adrenocortical hormones)

4. A marked decrease in the numbers of eosinophils (one kind of invasion-fighting white blood cell). Selye called this consistent pattern of response to stress the general adaptation syndrome (GAS).

According to Selye's studies, the GAS was divided into three stages: (1) the alarm reaction, (2) the stage of resistance, and (3) the stage of exhaustion. During the first, or alarm, stage the level of adrenocortical hormones in the bloodstream rises sharply, and those systems that are most suitable to handle the particular stress are called into play. At this point the resistance stage begins, and the level of adrenocortical hormones in the blood decreases. Now resistance to the specific stress is high, but the body's overall ability to withstand other stresses decreases: The individual may be well prepared to deal with extreme cold but is very vulnerable to a bacterial infection. If the stress is extreme or persists for a long time, the individual will enter the third, or exhaustion, stage. Now, as adrenocortical hormones rise once again, one of two outcomes is possible: Either another system is called into play to defend the body and help the individual adapt to the stress, or the individual, totally depleted, will succumb to the stress and die.

STRESS BEFORE SELYE

Selye's pioneering discovery of the GAS in rats forms the basis of and provides the conceptual framework for many subsequent studies of stress in animals and humans. But Selye's work resulted from earlier studies that were concerned with the body's ability to maintain physiological balance and its reactions to change. In particular, as Selye himself acknowledged, his research owed a great debt to two physiologists: Claude Bernard, a Frenchman; and Walter Bradford Cannon, an American. In the latter part of the 19th century, Bernard, working at the University of Paris, pointed out that the body has a *milieu intérieur*, an "internal environment," which it strives to maintain in a more or less constant state despite wide-ranging changes in the external environment. Fifty years later, Cannon, who taught at Harvard, described this dynamic equilibrium, or balance of forces within the organism, as "homeostasis" (from the Greek *homoios*, meaning "similar," and *stasis*, meaning "position").

Cannon also developed another perspective that would come to enlarge and enrich Selye's. He suggested that when confronted with particularly disturbing events in their environment, animals experienced a set of physiological changes that he characterized as the "fight-or-flight" response. This state of arousal and preparedness included the following manifestations: an increase in heart rate and rate of breathing; muscular tension; coldness and sweatiness; a decrease in intestinal activity; and a dilation, or increase, in size of the pupil of the eye. In this state the animal is primed to flee (as from a predator or a storm) or, if necessary, to fight.

Cannon's fight-or-flight response depended largely on the nervous system and its connections to the inner part of the adrenal gland, the medulla. When stimulated by a nervous system aroused by threatening external events, the adrenal medulla would manufacture the chemicals adrenaline (epinephrine) and noradrenaline (norepinephrine), which would in turn produce the manifestations of the fight-or-flight response. By contrast, Selye's GAS functioned primarily through the pituitary gland, which chemically controls the adrenal cortex and the structures of the immune system (thymus, lymph nodes, etc.). Later researchers would combine both of these perspectives and enlarge them to include many new findings about the complex relationship between the nervous, endocrine, and immune systems to produce the modern biological perspective on stress that will be discussed in the next chapter.

STRESS SINCE SELYE

In the years since Selye undertook his initial research, science's knowledge of the biology of stress has been complemented by an ever-broader and -deeper understanding of the psychological, social, and environmental factors that create and perpetuate stress in humans as well as in animals. As this knowledge has increased, so too have the factors implicated in stress production. Economic pressures, crime, social and psychological alienation, and threats to the environment have all proliferated, pushing the cumulative level of stress ever higher.

In the last 50 years these stressors, as well as the pathways through which they act, have been identified, classified, and quantified in a variety of ways. It is now known that death and divorce, a hateful job, or a crowded, crime-filled neighborhood can act on the brain as powerfully as poisons or physical pain, producing the biological changes that Selye and Cannon described.

It has also been discovered during the same period of time that these and other stressors play an important role in producing and maintaining the majority of the chronic debilitating conditions from which people in developed countries are likely to suffer. These illnesses include heart disease, arthritis, depression, asthma, insomnia, headaches, backaches, and cancer.

These studies on the causes of stress and on the kinds of personalities that are likely to develop particular illnesses have helped point the way to new methods for alleviating stress. For example, as investigators traced out the pathways by which emotional tension could be translated into a biological disturbance, some began to suspect that, conversely, feelings of emotional well-being could be instrumental in preventing or relieving a biological disturbance. Indeed, research has provided evidence for this theory: Positive emotional experiences, a variety of relaxation therapies including biofeedback, meditation, and positive mental imaging have all proved useful in reducing stress and alleviating stress-related illnesses.

Similarly, deliberate attempts to change one's attitude or social support system have been shown to have positive effects upon

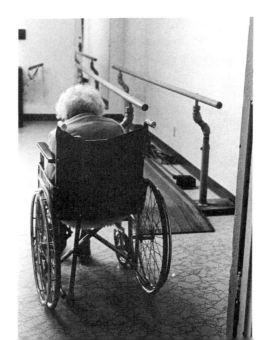

Isolation, often experienced by the elderly, is a major cause of stress and stress-related illness.

17

stress-related conditions. For example, widowers generally experience high levels of social alienation and loneliness. Both of
these feelings are now known to increase stress and make them
more vulnerable to heart attacks than are married men of the
same age and general status. Therefore, one health promotion
strategy that has been developed for these men entails more frequent contact with health care providers and membership in a
mutual support group in which potential cardiac patients are
committed to helping one another out. It turns out that more
contact with other people and a more positive attitude toward
life does seem to have some value in lowering the risk in widowers
of illness and premature death.

GOOD AND BAD STRESS

Although the major focus in stress research has been on the
experimental production and treatment of stress-related illnesses, Selye and those who followed him have also been interested in the creative aspects of stress and in the variable responses
of different people to the same kinds of stress.

Selye recognized early on that stress was a common factor of
all life as well as a potential contributor to illness. Stress was an
integral part of change, and change was, of course, the essence
of life, the force propelling people out of their family and into
the world, away from parents and siblings toward friends and
husbands and wives and children of their own. Growth and development could not exist without stress; nor could creativity or
innovation in art, science, or commerce; nor indeed could life
itself.

Selye distinguished between distress and eustress; both subsets
were characterized by the same apparent physiological reaction,
but one tended to lead to physical illness, whereas the latter
produced a state of well-being and satisfaction. The differences,
Selye recognized, were in the match between the stressor and
the person the stress affected; and, more particularly, in the dif-
fering attitudes of people subjected to the same stress. An elec-
toral campaign might be an overwhelming burden to a person
with an introverted, artistic temperament and a prolonged high
to a prospective officeholder; a rigorous exam could be seen as
a welcome experience by one student and as a frightening trauma

by another. These differences would be reflected in the individual's reactions to the common stressor.

In the last 50 years, researchers have elaborated and refined concepts of stress and its causation and the biological pathways by which it manifests itself (sometimes in ways that Selye and the other early researchers could not have imagined). At the same time, clinicians have used these discoveries to help them respond to the implied challenge that Selye issued some years ago. They are learning to focus more and more on humans' remarkable and newly rediscovered capacity to alter their physiological response and change their attitude to stress, to turn a potential threat into a challenge, to transform distress into eustress.

PSYCHOSOCIAL ASPECTS OF STRESS

At the beginning of the 20th century, decades before Selye formulated his theories about stress, Adolph Meyer, a professor of psychiatry at the Johns Hopkins Medical School, became aware of the profound effects of life changes on the occurrence and severity of physical as well as psychological problems. Meyer, who kept a "life chart" of his patients, discovered that illnesses of all kinds tended to occur at times when several significant changes occurred in a person's life.

Stressful Events

In the late 1940s, Thomas Holmes began to give a new dimension to the idea that certain occurrences could initiate stress. When he and his colleagues studied the events surrounding the occurrence of a new case of tuberculosis, or the lack of improvement in a chronic case, they were able to observe a consistent pattern: These changes in disease status were preceded by one or more life crises that the patients experienced as overwhelming and depressing. In time it became clear that some crises, some "life events," were more likely to accompany the onset or worsening of illness than others. When they broadened their investigation, Holmes and his co-workers discovered that there tended to be a cluster of these stressful life events around the onset of virtually every major, and many minor, illnesses.

By 1967, Holmes and his collaborator, Richard Rahe, then at the UCLA Medical Center, had made considerable headway in quantifying the potency of these life events. They developed what they called the Social Readjustment Rating Scale (modified later to the Schedule of Recent Events—SRE): some 43 events, listed in the order of their capacity to produce stress and to predispose an individual to illness. At the top of the list was death of spouse, valued at 100 points of stress production, followed by divorce (73) and marital separation from mate (65). Most of these events were regarded as bad or unfortunate, but, as Holmes and Rahe learned, apparently happy events, which brought with them great change, could also produce stress; for example, marriage was awarded 50 stress points and outstanding personal achievement, 28.

Holmes and Rahe observed that the effects of stress were cumulative. The more points one had on the scale, the more likely one was to develop an illness. Someone who scored 150 points during the previous 12-month period had a 50% likelihood of developing an illness; someone with 300 or more points had a 90% chance of falling ill.

In the last 20 years, Holmes and Rahe's scale and others modeled on it have been an effective way to evaluate stress levels and to predict the likelihood an affected person would have of developing an illness; 1 study of healthy young doctors in training, for example, revealed that 49% of those with 300 or more stress points in an 18-month period fell ill in the next 8 months, in contrast to only 9% of those with 150 to 199 stress points.

Stressed Personalities

In addition to these studies on the measurement of stressful events, a great deal of research has dealt with the attitudes that drive individuals to turn these events from challenges into disasters and on the personality characteristics that accompany and may produce specific stress-related illnesses. This work, which has been undertaken primarily by psychiatrists and psychologists, has been the foundation of science's growing understanding of the complex connections between social and emotional stress and specific disease states.

Two controversial pioneers in this area were Georg Groddeck and Wilhelm Reich, physicians who were greatly influenced by Sigmund Freud's psychoanalytic theories. Both Reich and Grod-

---

SOCIAL READJUSTMENT RATING SCALE

Rank	Life event	Mean value
1	Death of spouse	100
2	Divorce	73
3	Marital separation	65
4	Jail term	63
5	Death of close family member	63
6	Personal injury or illness	53
7	Marriage	50
8	Fired at work	47
9	Marital reconciliation	45
10	Retirement	45
11	Change in health of family member	44
12	Pregnancy	40
13	Sex difficulties	39
14	Gain of new family member	39
15	Business readjustment	39
16	Change in financial state	38
17	Death of close friend	37
18	Change to different line of work	36
19	Change in number of arguments with spouse	35
20	Mortgage over $10,000	31
21	Foreclosure of mortgage or loan	30
22	Change in responsibilities at work	29
23	Son or daughter leaving home	29
24	Trouble with in-laws	29
25	Outstanding personal achievement	28
26	Spouse begins or stops work	26
27	Begin or end school	26
28	Change in living conditions	25
29	Revision of personal habits	24
30	Trouble with boss	23
31	Change in work hours or conditions	20
32	Change in residence	20
33	Change in schools	20
34	Change in recreation	19
35	Change in church activities	19
36	Change in social activities	18
37	Mortgage or loan less than $10,000	17
38	Change in sleeping habits	16
39	Change in number of family get-togethers	15
40	Change in eating habits	15
41	Vacation	13
42	Christmas	12
43	Minor violations of the law	11

Thomas Holmes and Richard Rahe devised this chart to rank the degree of stress that certain events have on a person's life.

deck observed certain connections between unconscious emotional conflict, bodily posture, and specific diseases; for example, Reich was impressed that repressed sexual feelings and tense pelvic musculature were associated with a variety of pelvic problems in women, including menstrual irregularities and cancer.

Later investigators in *psychosomatic medicine* (from the Greek words *psyche*, "spirit" or "mind," and *soma*, "body"), including Franz Alexander, Helen Flanders Dunbar, and George Engel, tried to give scientific precision to the developing field.

Alexander, who taught at the Chicago Psychoanalytic Institute, was particularly interested in mapping the connections between unconscious emotional conflicts and specific stress-related illnesses. For example, he observed that stomach and duodenal ulcers (the duodenum is the first part of the small intestine) were common in men who had unmet needs for emotional dependency. He mapped out similar relationships between personality types and physical illnesses for such other conditions as arthritis and asthma.

Engel, on the other hand, became particularly interested in the general emotional state that might predispose someone to develop any of a variety of stress-related illnesses. In one study he noted that 59% of people who died suddenly had recently experienced a period of profound emotional loss or grief. Soon he and his colleague Arthur Schmale were observing a consistent connection between emotional states described as "despair," "giving up," and "grief" and the onset or exacerbation of "literally the whole range of organic disease," including heart attacks and cancer. These people, Engel and Schmale observed, tended to relate their feelings of hopelessness and helplessness to their own failures and to become stuck in a cycle of self-blame and disease.

APPLYING THE DATA

During the last 20 years, hundreds of researchers have worked to fill in the details of the picture that Cannon and Selye, Holmes and Rahe, Reich and Groddeck, and Alexander and Engel first sketched. What has so far emerged are detailed renderings of some elements in the psychosocial landscape and the beginnings of connections among them.

Here are some examples drawn from recent research on cancer: Caroline Thomas's psychological studies of Johns Hopkins medical students have demonstrated that students who experienced a profound "lack of closeness" to their parents when they were young were more likely than their classmates to develop cancer when they were older. Research by Lawrence Le Shan and others on cancer patients shows that a high percentage of these people developed their cancer during a period of extreme emotional stress, often related to a feeling of despair following a loss; most of them, it turned out, had suffered a traumatic emotional loss during childhood.

More recently, links have been forged between these and other psychosocial stressors and the biological changes that may lead

Dying Mother and Child, *by the Norwegian painter Edvard Munch. Losing a loved one—especially a parent—during childhood can cause a lifelong tendency toward depression and susceptibility to stress and illness.*

to cancer. Work by Marvin Stein and many others has shown that psychological states of grief and helplessness depress the immune system's production of the T cells and natural killer cells that destroy cancer cells. It seems that adverse psychosocial history, recent traumatic life events, and a depressed emotional state may collaborate with genetic predisposition and environmental insults in altering an individual's biology and preparing the way for disease, even cancer.

•   •   •   •

CHAPTER 2

· · · · · · · · · · · · · ·

THE BIOLOGY
OF STRESS

Adrenaline, the common name for the hormone epinephrine

Hundreds of investigators have mapped the many dimensions of stress since Selye did his pioneering research. They have discovered that stress has a wide variety of psychological causes and effects, some of which were touched on in Chapter 1, and social, economic, and ecological causes, which will be discussed in Chapter 3. But in one's immediate experience, stress is primarily a biological phenomenon, an intimate drama that is played out in everyone's body. It begins to take shape during infancy—even in the womb—and continues to affect people physically and emotionally throughout their life. It affects the most sophisticated parts of the body, such as the central nervous system, as well as the peripheral and autonomic nervous systems, and the endocrine and immune systems.

STRESS AND THE CENTRAL NERVOUS SYSTEM

Much of one's experience of stress is conscious. A person knows when he or she is worried about an upcoming exam or relationships with family or friends. This knowledge is expressed as thoughts and feelings, as changes in one's emotions and body. This experience of stress is registered in the central nervous system, most particularly, in the brain. The brain in turn sends signals, communicating one's mental state to all the other systems and organs in the body.

The brain is the most important organ in the central nervous system.

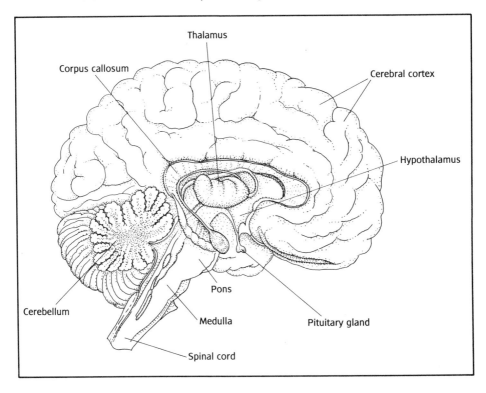

The central nervous system (CNS) is composed of the brain and the spinal cord. The CNS transmits information to and receives and integrates information from the sense organs (eyes, ears, nose, etc.), the peripheral nervous system (which registers touch, pain, position, heat and cold, etc.) and the autonomic nervous system (which governs such involuntary functions of the body as digestion, heart rate, respiratory rate, etc.).

The largest part of the CNS is the brain, an organ located within the skull and composed of perhaps 1 trillion cells and weighing 62.5 ounces. The brain can be divided into two major components—the cerebral cortex (the upper and outer part) and the subcortex (the lower part).

The lowest part of the subcortex, the medulla, is continuous with the spinal cord. It contains collections of neurons (nerve cells) that regulate such basic processes as the heartbeat and the number of times per minute a person breathes in and out. When a person feels stress, these centers are affected, with a resulting increase in the heartbeat and the rate of respiration. Above the medulla is the *pons* (Latin for "bridge"), which plays a major role in the sleep cycle, and above and behind it is the cerebellum, a structure concerned with coordinating bodily movement.

The *diencephalon* (also called the betweenbrain) lies above the pons and below the cerebral cortex. It consists of the basal ganglia, the thalamus, the hypothalamus, and, as one might expect, is concerned with transmitting messages between the spinal cord and the lower part of the brain and the cerebral cortex. In particular, the diencephalon communicates the person's needs, feelings, and sensations to the cerebral cortex and is in turn affected and regulated by the thoughts, memories, images, and commands of the cortex.

The thalamus is concerned particularly with conveying pain sensations. In Selye's experiments with physical trauma in animals, the thalamus (from the Greek *thalamos*, or "inner chamber") served as a way station, registering pain, activating the animal's conscious knowledge of it and contributing to the onset of the stress reaction. The hypothalamus (in Greek, *hypo* means "under"), a pea-sized structure weighing only an ounce or two, is probably the most complex part of the diencephalon. In recent years, researchers have begun to demonstrate how important it is in producing—and relieving—the manifestations of stress.

The hypothalamus contains important centers for pain and pleasure. It is the control center for the various functions of the autonomic nervous system, including heartbeat, blood pressure, respiratory rate, hunger, thirst, and sexual urges. The hypothalamus is also the part of the brain that integrates the information derived from the brain's higher structures— including thoughts and emotions—with the biological functioning of the organism. In a stressful situation, the disturbed thoughts and emotions that the cortex registers are translated into the biochemical messages and electrical signals by which brain cells communicate with one another. These messages and signals convey the presence of stress to the lower centers of the brain and from there to the autonomic nervous system, the endocrine system, the immune system, and the neuropeptide systems, which in turn send messages to the entire body, producing the physical symptoms of stress.

The hypothalamus links the higher, cortical parts of the brain to the master, or pituitary, gland, which in turn regulates the secretions of the endocrine system (thyroid gland, adrenal glands, sex glands, etc.) and the immune system. In the various specialized nuclei of the hypothalamus, impulses from cells in the cerebral cortex are translated into messages that are conveyed to the anterior and posterior lobes of the pituitary gland. One part of the hypothalamus (the anterior, lateral zone) inhibits both the sympathetic response of the autonomic nervous system (implicated in the fight-or-flight reaction) and the output of stress hormones from the pituitary, whereas another part of the hypothalmus (the posterior medial) stimulates the sympathetic nervous system and the release of stress hormones from the pituitary.

The next higher part of the brain is the *limbic* (from the Latin word for "border") system. The border is between the higher functions of the cortex, which are related to thought processes, and the lower structures, which are related to basic bodily processes. This system includes some of the thalamic and hypothalamic nuclei as well as parts of the frontal and temporal cortex. It is concerned with emotions and their expression and with the senses of hearing and smell. When the limbic system registers sounds or smells that are indicative of a dangerous situation—

or recalls unpleasant memories—it conveys these to the cortex, which in turn will initiate a stress response.

The uppermost portion of the brain is the cerebral cortex. The cortex is the area in which complex movements, abstract thinking, language, and judgment originate and in which complex verbal and visual memories are stored. It is the most highly developed part of the human brain and the part whose functioning most clearly marks us as humans. The cortex provides the final integrating site for information received outside the body and for the response to stress. Research has shown that memories are stored in many places in the cortex and that in situations where some parts of the brain have been damaged, other areas of the cortex are capable of taking over their functions.

Still, there is a high degree of specialization in the intact brain: The left frontal area of the organ is more concerned with logical thought, language, and speech, whereas the right side is specialized to deal with images, including one's image of his or her body, and artistic expression; the left side tends to analyze, the right to develop concepts describing general situations.

Artistic expression is governed by the right side of the brain.

All these areas of the brain are integrated in a variety of ways and connected by feedback loops that enable one part of the brain to exert a modifying influence on another. For example, when the thalamus registers physical pain, it sends signals to the cortex that initiate a stress response designed to help the individual cope with or escape from the pain. When the pain is relieved, signals travel back to the thalamus, instructing it to shut off the flow of information to the cortex.

One pathway for mutual influence is the corpus callosum, a structure that connects the right and left hemispheres of the cortex and helps to integrate visual with verbal intelligence; for example, it supplies the perception of a stressful sight with the words to describe it. Another integrating structure is the reticular activating system (RAS), a centrally located, vertical column of cells that provides a two-way pathway among the autonomic, subcortical, and cortical structures. The RAS helps discriminate between those novel or new stimuli that need to be brought to the attention of the higher structures and those that can be managed, out of conscious awareness, by the lower centers. It also transmits information from the cortex to these centers.

THE AUTONOMIC NERVOUS SYSTEM

When a man's heart is beating quickly, when his palms are sweaty and his muscles tense, he is receiving biological messages from the autonomic nervous system (ANS). These messages are conveying, insistently and emphatically, that the man is under stress.

The autonomic nervous system is so named because it relates to functions that seemed to early investigators to operate autonomously—below one's customary level of awareness and outside of conscious control—including heart rate, blood pressure, changes in size of the pupil of the eye and movement of the intestinal tract. During the last 25 years, however, scientific studies of highly trained Indian yogis who were able to regulate all of these functions have suggested that at least some people could control these autonomic functions. More recent work with stress reduction techniques, most particularly biofeedback, has shown that many people can be trained to control these functions consciously. Still, the name autonomic nervous system remains.

The ANS is divided into the sympathetic and parasympathetic nervous systems. The sympathetic nervous system (SNS) is concerned with arousal and outside activity, with expending energy, tensing muscles, and stimulating the endocrine system. It is the vehicle for the fight-or-flight reaction, which Cannon described, and comes into play in situations of stress. It is called sympathetic because it coordinates the functions that are mobilized in sympathy with activity. The SNS increases heart rate, blood pressure, and the secretion of sweat. It causes pupils to dilate and gastrointestinal movement to decrease. The affected person becomes hyperactive and tense. He or she may also have cold feet and clammy hands.

The parasympathetic nervous system (PNS), by contrast, relates to the more inward activities of the body, to functions concerned with relaxation, nourishment, and storing energy. When the PNS dominates, heart rate decreases, blood pressure goes down, sweating decreases, pupils constrict, and gastrointestinal functioning increases. The affected person becomes relaxed and drowsy.

The sympathetic and parasympathetic systems often have opposite effects. For example, fibers from sympathetic ganglia (collections of nerve cell bodies) near the upper back speed up heart rate by secreting norepinephrine at sites in the heart and blood vessels, whereas parasympathetic fibers from the large and long vagus nerve (from the Latin "to wander") slow heart rate. At other times the SNS and PNS act in concert: The PNS produces erection of the penis and the SNS governs ejaculation. In general however, the PNS provides the nourishment and stores the energy that will be expended as needed when the SNS is called into play.

The two systems are anatomically distinct. The highest centers of the SNS are in the hypothalamus. Its nerve fibers run on either side of the bony vertebrae of the spine and connect to cells in the ganglia. From these ganglia other fibers travel to the heart, lung, intestines, sweat glands, and adrenal medulla. They produce their effects in these organs by releasing epinephrine at their nerve endings. The adrenal medulla may be seen as a part of the SNS. When stimulated, it too releases epinephrine (as well as the chemically related norepinephrine), which in turn amplifies the effects of the SNS stimulation.

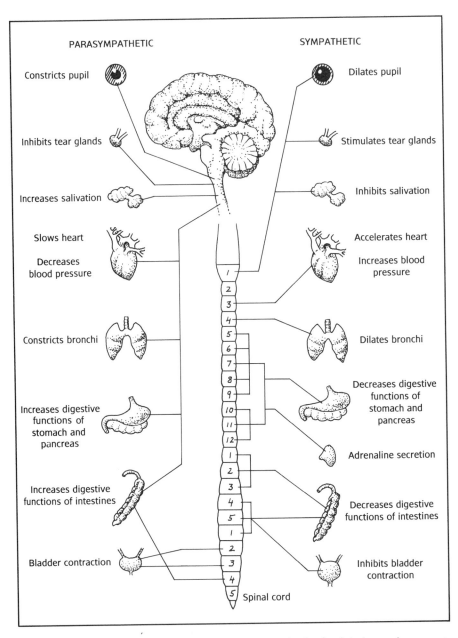

PARASYMPATHETIC

Constricts pupil

Inhibits tear glands

Increases salivation

Slows heart

Decreases
blood pressure

Constricts bronchi

Increases digestive
functions of
stomach and
pancreas

Increases digestive
functions of intestines

Bladder contraction

SYMPATHETIC

Dilates pupil

Stimulates tear glands

Inhibits salivation

Accelerates heart

Increases blood
pressure

Dilates bronchi

Decreases digestive
functions of
stomach and
pancreas

Adrenaline secretion

Decreases digestive
functions of intestines

Inhibits bladder
contraction

Spinal cord

The parasympathetic nervous system controls the body's inward activities; the sympathetic nervous system governs the body's reactions to the outside world.

The wide distribution of the SNS provides for a speedy and coordinated response suitable for the needs of an animal or a human living in the wild. In contemporary humans, the response may be overly intense—a kind of physiological overkill for the ongoing low-grade stressors that the contemporary urbanite may experience.

The PNS, by contrast, is capable of more discrete action. This follows from its anatomy. The PNS has a center in the brain close to the SNS, but its nerve fibers travel within, not outside of, the spinal cord. The fibers leave the vertebral column above and below those of the SNS, through the cervical vertebrae (located in the neck) and the lumbar and sacral vertebrae (located in the lower back).

Almost 80% of these PNS fibers are carried by the left and right vagus nerves. Both vagus nerves leave the brain from within the skull and journey downward, sending branches to the throat, lungs, heart, and stomach. The right vagus continues to supply branches to the small and large intestines. Other branches of the PNS emerge in the lumbosacral area and supply the bladder, the lower part of the large intestine, and the sexual organs. The ganglia of the PNS fibers are close to or within the structure of the organs they supply, thus helping this system to maintain its specificity. The postganglionic fibers of this system secrete the chemical acetylcholine at their nerve endings.

THE ENDOCRINE SYSTEM

The endrocrine system, because it plays a vital part in preparing all the cells in the body to cope with the demands of stress, was of primary importance to Selye in the research that helped him develop his theory of the GAS. The endocrine system includes the master gland (the pituitary) and the glands—the thyroid, adrenals, ovaries, testes, and that part of the pancreas concerned with sugar metabolism—that the pituitary regulates. Each of these glands secretes *hormones* (from the Greek *horme*, or "outflowing") into the bloodstream; all affect the body in a variety of complex ways; and all interact in a series of feedback loops with the central and autonomic nervous systems as well as with one another.

The pituitary, which is located at the base of the skull just below the hypothalamus, is divided into anterior and posterior portions. The anterior portion secretes *tropic* (from the Greek for "nourishing") hormones. These include somatotropic hormone (STH), which regulates body growth; adrenocorticotropic hormone (ACTH); thyrotropic hormone (TTH); and several gonadotropic hormones, which affect the genitals. The posterior pituitary discharges two hormones directly into the bloodstream: vasopressin, which promotes contraction of the walls of the arteries; and oxytocin, which contracts the muscle of the uterus. When a person is under physical or emotional stress, the cerebral cortex sends messages to the hypothalamus, which then produces "releasing factors" that stimulate the pituitary to secrete ACTH and TTH into the bloodstream.

ACTH, which is the primary pituitary hormone involved in the stress reaction, stimulates the cortex, or outer part of the adrenal gland, which in turn releases the glucocorticoid (blood- and sugar-raising) hormones, cortisone and cortisol; and the mineralocorticoid (salt-controlling) hormones, including aldosterone, which promote retention of sodium and chloride and excretion of potassium. The glucocorticoids also produce the anti-inflammatory response and the gastric ulcers noted by Selye; the mineralocorticoids, by contrast, promote inflammation. TTH, the other major pituitary stress hormone, causes the thyroid gland to secrete thyroxine, which increases the rate of cellular metabolism, or activity, throughout the body.

ACTH and TTH thus cooperate in preparing the body to meet the challenge of stress by making sugar available for cellular metabolism and by increasing the metabolic rate of the cells. They also increase heart rate, help conserve the body's water, and increase the individual's sense of power and well-being. ACTH and TTH also act to inhibit the secretion of STH and the gonadotrophins, neither of which is particularly helpful in meeting stress.

The effects of these hormones are further amplified by the epinephrine that the adrenal medulla releases. Epinephrine mobilizes glucose from the liver to provide energy for the cells whose metabolism has been stepped up by higher levels of thyroxine. Epinephrine also increases heart rate, elevates body temperature, and increases oxygen consumption.

The stress response of the endrocrine system, with its hormonal secretions and metabolic effects, is triggered by the brain's perception of stressful stimuli. It is also becoming clear that the released hormones can themselves exert direct effects on the brain. For example, it has recently been discovered that some hormones, including ACTH, have molecular receptors on brain cells to which they can attach. These receptors permit hormones to act in a feedback loop via the hypothalamus to control and modify the stress response that originally stimulated their production.

STRESS AND THE IMMUNE SYSTEM

When Hans Selye did his initial studies on stress he noted that the increase in adrenocortical hormones was accompanied by a decrease in the size of the thymus and lymph nodes, structures that are among those primarily responsible for producing the body's protective, or immune, response to invading bacteria and viruses. In recent years an enormous amount of research has been devoted to describing the structures and detailing the functioning of the immune system and its complex interaction with the central and autonomic nervous systems and the endocrine systems. Scientists have opened an entire new field of investigation—called psychoneuroimmunology—to study this interaction. It is now clear that there are several kinds of immunity and many different aspects to the immune system. With few exceptions, we are all born with "innate" immunity, which provides nonspecific defense against bodily invasion. The structures that produce innate immunity include the skin and the stomach (more precisely, the acids of the stomach), which provide, respectively, mechanical and chemical barriers against potentially harmful organisms, and the blood, which contains cells that are capable of destroying invaders that get past these barriers.

Among the most important of the infection-fighting white blood cells (so named because of their pale color when stained and examined under the microscope) are monocytes and neutrophils (neutral in color when stained). Neutrophils can directly attack invaders; when monocytes approach an area of bacterial or viral activity they are converted to *macrophages* (from the Latin for "big eaters"), large cells that are capable of ingesting invaders or tissue debris.

With few exceptions, every person is born with an innate immune system—the most prominent part of which is the skin—to protect against bacterial invasion.

Acquired immunity develops after the body is invaded and also depends on white blood cells. It is of two kinds: humoral and cellular. *Humoral* immunity (from the Latin for "fluid") depends on the production of a blood-borne protein, called an antibody, which is capable of destroying the specific invader, or antigen. Humoral immunity is provided by a white blood cell called the B lymphocyte, which originates in the marrow, or inner part, of some bones as a stem cell. Ultimately, it develops into a plasma cell, which is capable of synthesizing antibodies. Cellular immunity depends on the ability of white blood cells called T lymphocytes to destroy invaders directly. The T lymphocytes originate in the bone marrow as stem cells that travel to the thymus, where they undergo maturation.

In addition to these defenses against external invaders, the immune system has a "surveillance" mechanism, which protects the body from pathological internal changes. Perhaps the most important of these surveillance functions is the destruction of cancer cells. Macrophages, T lymphocytes, and B lymphocytes are involved in this process of surveillance and destruction as are cells called killer (K) cells, natural killer (NK) cells, and cytotoxic (cell-killing) T cells.

The primary sites of the immune system include the bone marrow, the thymus, the lymph nodes, the spleen, and collections of lymph tissue in the intestine called Peyer's patches, named after the Swiss anatomist who discovered them in the 17th century. The bone marrow is a primary cell-producing site, but the thymus seems to have a major role in monitoring, maturing, and modulating the cells responsible for the immune response.

It is now clear that both the thymus and marrow—and, to a lesser degree, the spleen and lymph nodes—interact directly with the CNS, the ANS, and the endocrine system in a variety of complex ways, many of which come into play in stressful situations. For example, under stress the cerebral cortex will send commands through the hypothalamus and the pituitary to the adrenal, which will produce corticoids that depress immune functioning. The hypothalamus also acts directly on the thymus to depress immune functioning (with a potential decrease in T cells, natural killer cells, etc.) and indirectly through neurotransmitters released by nerve endings of the ANS.

NEUROPEPTIDES

In recent years, researchers in brain biochemistry have begun to investigate a whole new class of compounds that are intimately involved in the stress response. These are called neuropeptides—peptides are structures composed of amino acids, the building blocks of proteins, and the prefix *neuro* refers to the fact that they were first found in the nervous system. These substances, of which more than 50 have been discovered, form a communication system that transmits information among the CNS, ANS, the endocrine system, and the immune system. Most, if not all, of them alter behavior and mood.

Two of the best known of the neuropeptides are the endorphins and substance P. The endorphins take their name from their capacity to produce responses that are similar to those created by the powerful narcotic and pain reliever morphine. When a person feels stress, these endorphins are released, creating a feel-

Running, when vigorously pursued, releases endorphins, which have a euphoric effect on the body similar to that of the narcotic morphine.

ing of well-being and blocking the pain response. Interestingly, they accomplish the latter task by interfering with the action of substance P, which facilitates transmission of pain impulses.

These and other neuropeptides are produced in the gastrointestinal tract as well as in the nervous system. Receptors for them appear at many locations, including the limbic system and hypothalamus in the brain, the spinal cord, and the gastrointestinal tract, as well as on the organs of the endocrine system and the cells of the immune system. This widespread distribution of receptors suggests that the neuropeptides may be a primary vehicle for integrating emotions and the biological processes they produce, including those that are involved in the stress response.

THE BIOLOGY OF STRESS: A CLINICAL OVERVIEW

The descriptions of the CNS, ANS, endocrine, immune, and neuropeptide systems only hint at their complexity, the degree to which all of these systems are integrated, and some of the ways in which each modifies the other. What follows is a highly oversimplified example of how a stressful event may affect each of these systems in a particular person, how they might then interact, and what the practical consequences might be.

Imagine preparing for a final exam in a course for which you have done very little of the work, one that is vitally important to your plans for the future. As you begin to pore over the required reading, you find that you will never be able to understand everything you need to. You begin to wonder if you will even be able to pass the exam.

The knowledge of your lack of preparedness, the possibility of impending failure, and all that it implies for your future are registered in the frontal and limbic areas of the cerebral cortex. The cortex sends neurochemical messages that the hypothalamus registers as fear and panic. The hypothalamus mobilizes itself to transmit electrical and chemical messages to the ANS, the immune system, and the anterior pituitary.

The ANS responds by stimulating the sympathetic nervous system. The SNS increases your heart rate and blood pressure, makes your muscles tense and your skin sweaty, and dilates your pupils. This response is augmented by messages that the ANS sends to the adrenal medulla, which secretes additional epinephrine and norepinephrine. You are now prepared to flee or to fight—or to sit at your desk studying for long, tense hours.

Meanwhile the hypothalamus is telling the anterior pituitary to secrete ACTH and TTH, which will in turn stimulate the adrenal cortex and the thyroid to release cortisone, cortisol, and thyroxine. The glucocorticoids mobilize sugar from your liver while the thyroxine gears up all of your body's cells to operate at a higher metabolic rate.

The effects of the stressful situation will also be transmitted to the organs and cells of the immune system, directly by the hypothalamus and indirectly by the actions of cortisone and cortisol. The cells of the immune system and its surveillance mechanism will be suppressed, making you more vulnerable to external invasion and less capable of controlling the production of abnormal cells in the body.

If the stress lasts only until you have taken the exam and then goes away, the body will soon recover. Heart rate, blood pressure, muscle tension, and cellular metabolism will all return to normal.

Homeostasis will be restored. The only unfortunate result may be a cold (from the temporary depletion of the immune system)—or a poor grade.

If the stress is prolonged or often repeated—if, for example, you are often unprepared and always in danger of failing and of disappointing yourself and your family—then changes in physical functioning may become as habitual as this psychological state. Now you may find yourself tense and sweaty even when you are not preparing for an exam.

If the situation persists long enough, and if it becomes a way of life rather than a reaction to a single stressor, then chronic functional change may lead to physical changes in the structure of the body and its organs and, ultimately, chronic physical illness. For example, the transient rises in blood pressure that accompany the stress response may become a permanent feature of your biology, leading to chronically constricted arteries and high blood pressure. At this point your chronic stress is beginning to produce a chronic stress-related illness called hypertension (high blood pressure), a condition that serves as the biological basis for many heart attacks and strokes.

•   •   •   •

CHAPTER 3
· · · · · · · · · · · · · ·
SOCIETAL AND ENVIRONMENTAL STRESSORS

S tress often appears as a result of personal circumstance; a divorce, a sad loss, or a tough exam may initiate disruptions in biological and psychological equilibrium. But it may also be provoked by any number of environmental and socioeconomic factors. Changes in season, temperature, and duration of daylight; in patterns of rainfall and the rise and fall of the stock market; in the tides and the phases of the moon; and in the way communities are organized and societies interact with one another are all elements that may act as stressors to which living things must accommodate themselves. The stress that human beings experience and the need they have to adjust themselves to changes in the environment are in many ways similar to the stress that other living things experience. They are also, in some important ways, quite different.

The similarities are fairly obvious. No creature on earth is immune to the changes in both the natural and man-made worlds. The differences turn on two complementary poles. On the one hand humans have far greater ability to adapt to or, indeed, to control, their external environment than do other animals. People can remove the external threat of winter cold by heating homes and putting on warm clothes and relieve the frantic search for food in dry years by effectively preserving and storing what has been harvested in fertile ones. Moreover, humans have a consciousness that other animals do not: a capacity for planning and imagining what might be, for reflecting on who they are and what they have done, and for changing the environment to conform to imaginings and desires.

On the other hand, the capacity humans have for complex mental functioning and the enterprise made possible by their creativity have helped to destroy the natural environment at the same time as they have enriched it. Humans have, after all, produced a polluted, time-pressured, overcrowded, lonely, inequitable, endangered world, which contributes in such a major way both to stress and to the anxious, fearful attitudes stress produces.

ECOLOGICAL FACTORS AND STRESS

For hundreds of years, humans have exploited the natural world for personal gain. In their anxiety to have as much as possible as fast as possible, people have taken from the earth what they believed they needed, with little thought either for the depletion of resources or the consequences of these efforts. Humans have treated the natural world as an object to be manipulated and exploited at will. In so doing, they have profoundly altered the ecological system.

There is a high price for such treatment. Disappearing species due to obliteration of grazing lands, worldwide pollution, famine, and ugliness represent the visible toll. The personal costs are apparent in the incredible proliferation of environmentally caused and stress-related illnesses: At present some 90% of illnesses for which people seek help, such as hypertension, asthma, and migraines, fall into these categories.

The signs of the ecological crisis, the "ecocidal" changes that are heightening stress, are everywhere. In their 1988 report "The State of the World," the Worldwatch Institute presented some of the alarming facts. In 1984, the warming of the earth via the greenhouse effect and the depletion of the earth's protective ozone layer (from the production of the chlorofluorocarbons used as propellants in aerosol sprays) seemed like real but remote concerns. Today, the hole in the ozone layer over Antarctica is twice the size of the continental United States and is growing quickly. Meanwhile, the unregulated use of fossil fuels like oil and coal continues to increase the amount of carbon dioxide (and other gases) in the earth's atmosphere, threatening to raise the earth's temperature far more quickly than scientists had expected.

The depletion of the ozone layer and the consequent increase in ultraviolet radiation reaching the earth from the sun are threatening to decrease crop output and drastically increase the incidence of skin cancer and eye damage. Meanwhile, the warming produced by the greenhouse effect could cause melting of polar ice caps, expansion of water in the ocean, and evaporation of moisture from the soil. These changes would have profound effects on agriculture, turning some farmland into desert (in such areas as the North American Midwest and the grain-growing regions of the Soviet Union) and causing other fertile lands (for example, the low-lying rice fields of Southeast Asia) to disappear under the sea.

These climatic threats to health and agriculture are compounded by the effects of pollution on air, rain, and soil. For example, the fourfold increase in the use of fossil fuels (and the lack of adequate controls over their emission when burned) between 1950 and 1979 brought, along with improvements in agriculture and transportation, an astonishing increase in carbon

Pollution brings stress into our life, destroying natural conditions and causing disease.

by-products and sulfur dioxide. These chemicals, transported by air currents and contained in precipitation, have produced the horrors of acid rain—thousands of lakes all over the world without fish or plant life, whole forests destroyed. To these stresses on the world's life-support systems are added the needs of an ever-expanding population for food and fuel whose cultivation and consumption further deplete forests, fresh water, and fertile land.

No one knows how great the effects of this global environmental stress on individuals are or will be, but there are already some early warnings. Small areas where neglect has been particularly great and pollution especially dangerous—like Love Canal, a neighborhood in Niagara Falls in western New York State where the Hooker Chemical Company created a chemical dump that eventually contaminated a school and housing tract—have had to be evacuated and have received much publicity. But there are far larger, and less well-known areas, like Czechoslovakia's heavily industrialized northern Bohemia, where the health consequences are as alarming and the implications as ominous. According to the Worldwatch Institute, the incidence of skin disease, stomach cancer, and mental illness in this part of the country is twice that of other sections of Czechoslovakia, and the life expectancy is 10 years shorter.

SOCIOECONOMIC ASPECTS OF STRESS

Human beings exploit not only the earth but also one another. At least since the breakdown of tribal societies, some human beings have tended to accumulate property and wealth beyond their immediate needs, to make use of the labor of others, and to enrich themselves at the expense of both other people and the environment. The Industrial Revolution, which brought immense changes to Europe and the United States in the late 18th and 19th centuries, accelerated this process, for it tended to centralize wealth and to concentrate populations in urban areas as well as to tax the environment.

The apologists for industrialism and capitalism were convinced that resources were all but inexhaustible; that wealth would trickle down and spread out; and that science, technology, and entrepreneurship would solve all environmental, social, and economic problems. Of course, this has not been the case. There is a higher level of material consumption and comfort among many in the developed world, but there are also high levels of poverty—as much as 20% of all Americans are inadequately nourished and hundreds of thousands are homeless. Nor has communism, which is the political philosophy of China, the Soviet Union, and much of Eastern Europe, been the universal salvation that its proponents hoped.

The world today is witnessing a disparity between the rich and the poor that is, if anything, greater than it ever has been. This is true on the international level, where the gap between the developed countries and many of the undeveloped countries grows wider each year. It is also true within many of the developed countries. In the United States, for example, many middle-class families have moved out of cities and into affluent suburbs,

The economic condition of poverty is often accompanied by such stresses as malnutrition and has grown worse as indigent segments of society have grown poorer.

leaving the inner city divided between the isolated enclaves of the very wealthy and the fragmenting ghettos of the very poor; meanwhile, the rural population has declined significantly, and the integrity of farm and ranch life has been broken. These divisions are emphasized by race: The wealthy, worldwide and within many nations, tend to be white; the poor are often black, Hispanic, and Asian.

SOCIAL SUPPORTS AND STRESS-RELATED ILLNESS

Both of these sweeping socioeconomic changes and many far smaller ones have had and continue to have an impact on the stress level—and the health—of the affected populations. In the 1960, Dr. Harold Wolff discovered that East Indians who made rapid changes in their socioeconomic status and were deprived of the supports of traditional village and family life experienced a far higher incidence of such stress-related illnesses as asthma and colitis than poorer people who remained in their traditional social and economic situation. Similar conclusions were drawn from research done on Navajos in the Southwest region of the United States.

These studies revealed that those who were displaced from their reservation developed tuberculosis at a far higher rate than those who remained on the reservation.

More recently, Dennis Jaffe compared health statistics from two neighboring states—Utah and Nevada—in the American West. Utah has the lowest incidence of hypertension and cardio-vascular disease, infectious diseases, and infant mortality in the United States. Nevada is at or near the top of the list in these ailments. The difference, according to Jaffe, is the result of the states' strikingly different social structures and life-styles: 72% of the residents of Utah are adherents of Mormonism, a religion that emphasizes "family ties and community obligations," con-tinuity, and stability; in Nevada, by contrast, much of the pop-ulation is highly mobile, and the social and community supports are far less strong—gambling, fueled by alcohol use and fraught with stress, is the chief industry.

In the last several decades, research attention has focused on the details of social support systems and the very real dangers to physical and emotional health that are produced when indi-viduals are deprived of these foundations. A 1962 study of Italian immigrants and their descendants who lived in a tight-knit, mu-tually supportive community in Roseto, Pennsylvania, is a good example. The study revealed that in spite of the high intake of animal fat and widespread obesity (both factors implicated in heart disease), Roseto residents were far less likely to develop heart attacks than their neighbors; a follow-up study indicated that Roseto inhabitants who left their community, with its social and emotional supports, began to experience heart attacks at the same rate as their neighbors.

More recently, the psychologist James Lynch has studied the effects of interpersonal loss and social alienation on the occur-rence of heart disease. In one of his studies, Lynch examined the effect of ordinary interpersonal situations on the blood pressure of healthy students. Those who had their blood pressure taken by a young man dressed in blue jeans who said he was a graduate student had significantly lower readings than students who had their blood pressure taken by this same man when he was dressed in a white coat and introduced himself as a doctor. Lynch concluded that the feelings of estrangement and fear prompted by the appearance of the white-coated, high-status "doctor" caused the rise.

In his book *The Language of the Heart*, Lynch summarizes research that puts his own and other experiments in a larger context. It is clear from these studies that loss or absence of any one of a number of sustaining relationships, and the emotional pain and stress that follow, can have serious physical consequences. The death of a spouse, lack of close family ties, feelings of alienation from one's immediate community, and even the absence of a comforting pet all predispose people to develop high blood pressure and die from heart disease.

WORK AND STRESS

The same destructive effects are apparent in people who feel overwhelmed by, alienated from, or dissatisfied with the work they are doing. One study of tax accountants revealed a strong correlation between their own subjective feelings of stress, an increase in their blood cholesterol levels (a high cholesterol level may be both a sign of stress and a precursor of heart disease), and the enormous increase in work that comes in the weeks prior to the April 15 deadline for filing taxes. Another study showed that people who experienced heart attacks were far more likely than others of the same age and socioeconomic status to do excessive amounts of work, to feel angry at those who slowed them down, and to be dissatisfied with their job.

Lack of interest in one's work, as well as overwork, can cause serious health problems. Studies done on more than 2,000 men in the 1970s by the Institute for Social Research in Ann Arbor, Michigan, revealed a high correlation between interest in one's work and level of health. For example, family doctors who worked long hours and had high levels of responsibility but were interested in their work had low levels of depression and anxiety and few incidents of physical illness. Assembly-line workers who

A truck driver expresses his anger over rising fuel prices. Low income and economic insecurity are major stressors.

had regular hours and good pay but undemanding and uninteresting jobs felt they were bored, became irritated easily, and were frequently ill.

STRESS AND POVERTY

The studies cited above indicate the deleterious effect of social dislocation and occupational stress, even when they are accompanied by economic well-being. It is also abundantly clear, however, that both low income and economic insecurity are major causes of stress and the illnesses to which it predisposes people. Studies done by Sidney Cobb on auto workers who were about to be fired revealed a marked increase in hypertension, ulcers, and arthritis, while Harvey Brenner's epidemiological research showed a consistent correlation between periods of economic recession and the incidence of cardiovascular disease, depression, and alcoholism.

The health status of those who must cope with chronic urban poverty—and the accompanying stresses of crime, overcrowding, inferior education, racial discrimination, and poor nutrition—is even more seriously compromised. Life expectancy is significantly less, and the incidence of virtually every kind of chronic illness—from heart disease to asthma and diabetes—is far higher among the urban poor than it is in more affluent populations.

•   •   •   •

CHAPTER 4

STRESS-RELATED ILLNESS

S tress-related illness is a condition that is characterized by an exaggeration and prolongation of one or more of the body's reactions to stress. Put another way, it is a transformation, over time and under continual pressure, of a normal stress response into a chronic condition. The particular condition or the "preferred system" (cardiovascular, gastrointestinal, etc.) that is affected is determined by a complex mixture of genetic, psychological, ecological, and socioeconomic forces, which were discussed in the first three chapters.

Because the stress response is so complex and involves so many systems, the variety of illnesses to which stress may contribute is enormous. Among the conditions generally thought to be stress related are hypertension, heart attacks, strokes, cancer, diabetes, asthma, arthritis, insomnia, obesity, anorexia, and depression—virtually all of the major illnesses that affect people in economically developed countries. Hypertension provides an excellent illustration of the relationship between the way people live and the stress they experience, between the biology of stress and the development of stress-related illness.

In the United States alone as many as 60 million people are estimated to have hypertension, that is, a blood pressure greater than 160/95 millimeters of mercury (normal is approximately 120/80). Hypertension is the major predisposing factor in the incidence of cardiovascular disease. And cardiovascular disease, which is the primary killer of people in all developed countries, is responsible for more than half the deaths in the United States each year and costs as much as $80 billion annually in medical expenses and losses in productivity.

Ninety percent of the people with hypertension have not had any preexisting disease—such as kidney disease or tumor of the adrenal medulla—that would have elevated their blood pressure. Their hypertension and the cardiovascular disease it may cause are intimately connected with stress, with the way they live and think about life, and with the world they live in.

THE LIFE AND HARD TIMES OF A
TYPE A PERSONALITY

In the 1970s, two San Francisco cardiologists, Meyer Friedman and Ray Rosenman, developed a composite picture of the typical patient with heart disease. (Friedman and Rosenman have also studied female Type A personalities, who may suffer more stresses than men do because they often have 40 or more hours of housework or caring for a family on top of their business-day work load.) A man ruled by the American ethic of achievement and toughness, committed to getting ahead in the world and doing it as fast as possible; resentful of the demands made upon him but unable or unwilling to do anything to relieve them; outwardly charming, especially to superiors, but inwardly resentful; tense, loud voiced, and prone to smiling nervously, at home as well as at the office. This is the man who is likely to develop hypertension and, when stressed sufficiently or for a long enough time, to succumb to heart disease or stroke. Friedman and Rosenman called this kind of man the Type A personality.

Friedman and Rosenman contrasted the Type A with the easygoing Type B personality. The Type B may hold the same kind of demanding job as the Type A, but he seems to enjoy it more and to be less preoccupied with his achievements or how others view him. He may even work the same long hours as the Type A, but he knows how to relax, by himself and with others, when he is not working.

What follows is a composite sketch of a Type A personality and a picture of a few of the stresses he feels. It will illustrate some of the pathways by which environmental stressors, social behavior, and the individual attitudes described above may be translated into the biological processes characteristic of stress, and, ultimately, physical disease.

Imagine a hard-charging executive, constantly working under deadlines, trying to produce more, eager to please his bosses in the organization and to squeeze as much work as possible from those under him. This is a man determined to do his job not only well but better than anyone else. He is a man under constant pressure, both from his work and from his ideas about how he should impress his superiors. This man—let us call him Fred— is determined to be cool and confident on the outside, and yet he is constantly worried and insecure inside. Eventually he will become resentful of all the work he is doing and the pressure he feels to do it. But, feeling trapped, he will not be able to do anything about it—except perhaps to take it out on those at work who are not in a position to argue with him and on his wife and children.

Fred's stress response will be more or less chronically activated. It will be transmitted from the cerebral cortex (where he thinks about himself and his work and how he is maintaining his image) to the limbic system (where emotions such as fear and anger are mixed with ideas), to the hypothalamus, and on to the ANS and the endocrine, immune, and neuropeptide systems.

The hypothalamus sends messages to the SNS, which secretes epinephrine, thus increasing the heart rate and raising blood pressure; SNS messages to the adrenal medulla further increase the levels of epinephrine and norepinephrine in the blood. The hypothalamus also commands the pituitary to release ACTH and TTH and to inhibit the release of STH and GSH (gonadotropin-stimulating hormone). ACTH causes the adrenal gland to secrete glucocorticoids and mineralocorticoids. The former mobilize sugar from the cells; the sugar in turn requires epinephrine as well as insulin for its metabolism; the latter hormones cause retention of sodium and chloride (the ingredients of common table salt), which increases the volume of fluid within the blood vessels and may contribute to hypertension. TTH stimulates the thyroid to produce thyroxine, which increases the metabolic rate and also the demands on the heart to pump blood.

A picture begins to emerge in which Fred's biology and psychology and his social role and the worldview of his society, mirror and reinforce one another. An angry, work-obsessed, emotionally repressed man, he is punishing himself physically and emotionally in order to conform to the competitive values and material goals of American society. Just as humans have exploited the natural world and ignored the disastrous effects on it, so Fred is exploiting his own productive energy and ignoring the damage he is inflicting. Over time the consequences will become clear, as Fred's state of chronic physiological arousal becomes the chronic stress-related illness called hypertension.

Fred's high blood pressure will put a further strain on a heart that is already taxed by an elevated heart rate and by the need to provide nourishment for cells that must achieve a higher metabolic rate. Chronic elevation of blood glucose, and the strain this puts on the pancreas, makes him more vulnerable to develop diabetes, which may further contribute to the development of heart disease. Meanwhile, his high level of circulating epinephrine makes him more irritable and less likely to sleep well, and his decreased levels of GSH may lower his sex drive.

The characteristics that combined to increase Fred's level of stress—his obsession with work and others' opinions, his insecurity, anxiety, and irritability—and to produce his hypertension

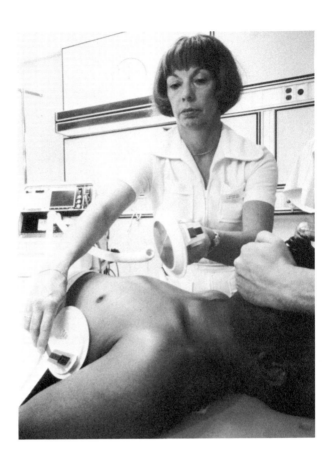

A doctor uses a defibrillator to revive a failing heart. This organ often bears the brunt of Type A stress.

are now amplified by the biological changes that his stress response has produced. Moreover, the means by which he tries to cope with his stress and his biological response to it may turn out to aggravate rather than relieve his condition.

Meals taken on the run or with demanding clients will strain his cardiovascular and digestive systems. So too may the content of the "power lunches" with which he tries to impress important clients: Refined foods and sugary desserts will increase the demand for circulating epinephrine and insulin; fatty foods—large portions of meat and sauces made with cream and butter —will lead to the production of high levels of cholesterol that will in turn predispose him to the development of fatty plaques in arteries already constricted by tension.

Unable to still a mind preoccupied with worry, Fred will almost certainly have difficulty sleeping at night. When he becomes fatigued enough, he will also have trouble staying awake during the day. If he resorts to large doses of alcohol to relax, as so many Type A's do, he will produce more strain on his heart and depress the functioning of his brain cells as well as injure his liver. If he uses large amounts of caffeine or nicotine to produce an alert, high-energy state during the day, he will increase his level of circulating epinephrine, produce more constriction of his arteries, and increase his heart rate and blood pressure.

Because he feels so pressed for time, so pressured to produce, it will be hard for Fred to spend time relaxing with his wife or children. Because he is so concerned with the opinions of others, it will be hard for him to be close to or confide in anyone. Rather than admit his vulnerability, he is likely to criticize his family members for theirs, to pressure them to produce more at their work or school or at home. The more he complains and nags and bullies, the more distance they will take from him, and the more isolated and put upon he will feel.

In his desperation to continue to produce, to be the man he thinks he should be, the man whom he wants others to see, he will do his best to avoid looking at the attitudinal causes of his stress, at the problems he is creating for himself and others, and at the possibility of changing how he works and lives. Instead of questioning or changing what he is doing, he may well ask his physician to prescribe drugs to help him continue the same self-destructive behavior.

Fred will tell his physician that he is experiencing symptoms of tension, insomnia, and anxiety. The physician will find a persistently elevated blood pressure and a rapid heart rate as well as a high level of cholesterol. Perhaps his doctor will suggest that Fred make some changes in his diet and life-style. Perhaps he will not. But in most cases he will not insist that this man take a look at his whole life—the way he works, how he relates to his family, and his responsibility for his problems. Instead, he is likely to treat the symptoms rather than the causes of the stress, to prescribe drugs for the hypertension and the cholesterol and tranquilizers, antidepressants, or sleeping pills (or even a combination of these) for the disturbed emotional state.

The drugs may work to keep Fred going. Probably his blood pressure readings will go down. For a time, at least, he may be able to sleep better at night and feel more relaxed at work. But

People often use—and abuse—alcohol to relieve stress.

the cause of his illness and unhappiness—his stress—will continue, and his stress-related hypertension, only temporarily masked, will progress. Meanwhile, the drugs will be exerting their own potentially dangerous side effects. Diuretics, which remove excess fluid and are often the first drug used to treat hypertension, may eventually cause damage to the kidneys. Tranquilizers, antidepressants, and sleeping pills—all of which have some potential for addiction—may increase the quantity of Fred's sleep but interfere with its quality. They may also further irritate his heart and depress or disturb his immune and digestive systems.

Because the sources of Fred's stress, his attitudes and the way he lives, are unchanged, his condition may well worsen. He is abusing his body and mind, indeed his very life, for small satisfactions and short-term gains, distorting his connections to other people and neglecting his own welfare. Uninformed by greater understanding of what he is doing to himself and why, unchecked by wiser counsel, he is headed for disaster: The biological catastrophes—the heart attacks and strokes—that high blood pressure can produce, the emotional disaster of marital unhappiness, the spiritual disaster of a joyless, driven life.

•　　　•　　　•　　　•

CHAPTER 5
· · · · · · · · · · · · · ·
THE STRESSES OF ADOLESCENCE

One of the stresses—and pleasures—of adolescence is the discovery of the opposite sex.

Adolescence (from the Latin *adolescere*, "to grow up") begins with the biological changes of puberty and culminates in the assumption of an adult's role and status. Prior to the beginning of the 19th century, adolescence seems hardly to have existed: All but the most privileged children immediately entered the world of work and marriage upon reaching puberty. In the last 200 years, in Western Europe and the United States, however, adolescence has been regarded as a distinct and distinctly stressful stage of life. In the early years of this century, the pioneering psychologist G. Stanley Hall wrote that this period was uniquely fraught with "storm and stress."

This perspective has subsequently been reinforced by most psychologists and psychiatrists as well as by a huge outpouring of popular writing and a consensus among parents. In the last three decades, however, it has come under some scrutiny. In *Growing Up in New Guinea* and *Coming of Age in Samoa*, the anthropologist Margaret Mead suggested that the stress of adolescence was a product of developed society, of the ever-lengthening period it has allowed to adolescence, and the confusion about how to deal with people going through this transition. The storm and stress were, she maintained, a sign of cultural distress, not a universal feature of adolescence; adolescence was inherently no more stressful than other developmental periods—infancy, middle age, old age. Others, including the American psychiatrist Daniel Offer, a specialist on adolescence, have raised similar questions.

Still, there is no question that adolescence is marked by profound biological, psychological, and social changes that set it apart from earlier and later stages of life, that it is a period of time in which life-shaping choices are made.

THE ADOLESCENT'S CHANGING BODY

The first and most obvious manifestations of adolescence are physical changes. They are initiated and controlled by the hypothalamus and pituitary gland, which alter levels of sex and growth hormones, and produce changes in primary and secondary sex characteristics. Primary sex characteristics are those that relate directly to the act of sexual intercourse; during adolescence the external genitalia, the ovaries, and testes mature. The changes in secondary sex characteristics include development of the breasts and hips in the female, growth of facial hair and deepening of the voice in the male, and growth of axillary (underarm) and pubic hair in both sexes.

With each generation, improvements in nutrition and other less clearly defined factors hasten the onset of puberty. At present, females begin puberty at an average age of 12 and males at 14, but the earliest secondary sex characteristic—the breast bud in females—may be present at age 8. In developed countries, there is an enormous range in the onset of puberty: Some girls may begin to have periods at 10, and others may not menstruate until 16; boys experience a spurt in growth and enlargement of their penis and testicles at any time between 12 and 17.

The biological changes of puberty can be tremendous sources of stress. The changes in hormonal levels influence the brain, which precipitates them, and interact with all the other components of the stress response—the ANS and the endocrine, immune, and neuropeptide systems—in a variety of ways that are both baffling and complex. The combination of these factors is partly responsible for the intense mixture of sexual urgency and discomfort that so often characterizes early adolescence.

To this volatile brew are added society's strangely mixed feelings about sexuality: It is highly touted in advertising, television, and movies, yet it is publicly disapproved of, presented as a sacred and exclusive experience in churches and synagogues, and trivialized and vulgarized in the press. The variability in onset of puberty further complicates the situation, making some young people feel either sexually retarded or uncomfortably precocious.

THE PSYCHOLOGY OF ADOLESCENCE

During adolescence, the brain, like the rest of the body, continues to develop. It increases in size and weight, myelinating (putting down a protective fatty myelin sheath around nerve fibers) a number of new areas including the reticular activating system (RAS), which is so vital to establishing connections between cortical and subcortical structures. This increase in size and complexity undoubtedly contributes to the adolescent's enhanced intellectual abilities and greater emotional range.

Most notable among the intellectual gains is the capacity for a greater degree of abstract thinking. Abstract thinking involves the ability to generalize from specific cases, to develop and test hypotheses, to understand and use symbols, and to put oneself in the place of another. These abilities make it possible for an adolescent to become concerned with all of the questions that preoccupy philosophers, scientists, artists, and religious thinkers: Who am I? Why are we here? How do things work? How can I best express myself? Does it all make sense? The combination of intellectual sophistication and creative imagination also provides the basis for the adolescent's moral concerns. It is at this time of life that most people begin to identify consciously with the plight as well as the achievements of others, to make commitments to ethical causes, political ideologies, and social movements.

The physical and mental changes of adolescence—the sudden surge in hormones and the remarkable growth in intellectual ability—are influenced by, and in turn shape, the emotional concerns of teenagers. Feelings for other people or ideas are intense, points of view passionately held. Attractions are swift, often overpowering, and stunningly changeable. Friendships that seemed undying dissappear in the storm of a quarrel; decisions made "forever" evaporate in an afternoon discussion. The adolescent is experimenting—with his or her body, with other people, with ideas about the world and the roles one can play in it.

Though each adolescent is unique, and adolescence itself varies widely from one place and time to another, certain developmental tasks or challenges are constant. Foremost among these is the development of what psychoanalyst Erik Erikson described as an "identity," a sense that one is a particular person with unique gifts and personality, a person functioning in the world and relating to other people. Erikson emphasized the connections between this individual sense of identity and the young person's feeling for himself or herself as a member of a society: Identity depends on interaction and identification with others, on a capacity to see oneself as rooted in a particular group or role in a specific historical context.

The other essential tasks of adolescence—the definition of oneself as apart from as well as a part of one's birth family and the development of intimacy with others—are intimately connected to the establishment of an identity and to one another. Both are gradual processes but may involve considerable uncertainty and oscillation. The adolescent boy who is rebelling against his parents' conservatism in religion, politics, and sexuality may, if he gets in trouble, find himself desperate for their practical help and emotional support. Similarly, the teenage girl who continually insists on doing "what all the other girls can do," may, when she is hurt by one of those girls, turn once again to her mother for comfort and reassurance.

One feature of adolescence is the development of an identity, a blend of individual style and manner.

THE STRESSES OF CONTEMPORARY LIFE

Each culture—and each historical period in that culture's evolution—provides a unique soil that nourishes and shapes the growth and development of its adolescents. And, of course, each culture has its own peculiar stresses. The developed nations, in the last years of the 20th century, provide a complex mix of nourishment and stress and opportunity and danger that is probably unmatched in all of human history.

The environmental, socioeconomic, and psychological stressors that affect adults also affect adolescents. Depending on their individual psychology, their socioeconomic situation, and the opportunities available to them, they may respond in ways that are quite different but still characteristic of adolescence. One adolescent's sense of idealism, her capacity for enthusiastic commitment, and her interest in defining herself through group mem-

Two men take part in a Sydney, Australia, AIDS vigil. As many adolescents mature, they begin to show concern for important causes and issues.

bership, may enable her to become a dedicated member of an environmental movement. Another girl's feeling of vulnerability and uncertainty, her dissatisfaction with the values and actions of the older generation, may make her feel discouraged about doing anything and negative about her own prospects; she may become withdrawn from her peers or join a group or gang whose members feel as disillusioned as she does.

Some aspects of life in developed countries in the late 20th century cast a shadow over the future of all adolescents. Obvious examples, in addition to environmental destruction, are the threats of nuclear war and of AIDS. Surveys of young people in the United States, Europe, and the Soviet Union reveal an all but universal feeling of dread about "the bomb"—a sense that sooner or later it will be used—and a feeling, at least intermittently, of hopelessness about the prospect.

If nuclear annihilation is the uncontrollable external peril, AIDS is the intimate enemy. It threatens the growing sexuality of adolescents, the area of their life that is often the most problematic as well as potentially the most pleasurable.

Other concerns, though universal, have a different weight for adolescents, who in different situations react to them in various ways. Many of these issues are principally connected with the hallmarks of adolescence—the biological changes of puberty, the development of independence from parents, and the need to define one's relationship with one's peers. Others relate more obviously to the larger socioeconomic forces that impinge on young people.

Because most adolescents live at home until they graduate from high school, their attempts to define themselves as separate and different from their parents inevitably create some conflict. This conflict often revolves around the adolescents' demands for independence and the parents' desire to protect them from the possible consequences of their actions. This "normal" conflict can, however, become extremely stressful and even destructive if all parties are not sensitive to its posssible ramifications.

Sometimes, the ordinary difficulties parents have in letting their children grow up become magnified. Instead of trying to let go gracefully, they become more intent on controlling their childrens' behavior. This may spark a rebellion in the adolescent and in turn create an escalating cycle of control and resistance. Alternately, if the parents are particularly powerful and the young person is not, they may encourage submissive, depressed, and dependent behavior in their child.

Parents who are insensitive to their child's need for continuing support and structure can create other problems: The teenager, who wants to be respected and cared for even while he or she is becoming more independent, will devise provocative and sometimes self-destructive behaviors to attract his or her parents' attention; if they fail to respond, he or she may decide to escalate this behavior in order to attract attention. In all these cases, parental attitudes and actions and the behaviors adolescents devise to deal with them combine to increase the young person's total level of stress.

Relationships with peers are crucial in helping the adolescent develop a sense of identity, but they may also, because of their importance, be a major source of stress. Here again, a certain amount of stress—apprehension about being accepted by others, conflicts about which group to identify with, the ups and downs of friendships and romantic relationships—is inevitable. Prob-

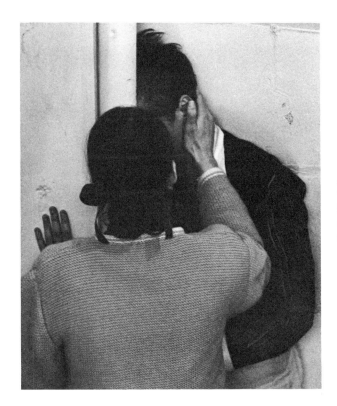

Developing relationships with peers is an important part of adolescence, but it can also be a source of stress.

lems with peer relations are much more serious when the young person either feels that there is no choice but to identify with and join a group whose behavior is itself destructive and delinquent, or when he or she feels so different and alienated that he or she is incapable of making friends or identifying with any group.

To these common stresses are added others that are both more directly connected with the larger socioeconomic and political forces and more variable in their impact. These include the effects of racial and sexual prejudices, the norms of behavior and the opportunities available in different communities, and changing patterns in employment and the economy. For example, in a time of economic uncertainty, when the disparity between the poor and the wealthy is growing larger, when there is a heightened emphasis on individual self-sufficiency, every adolescent is going to be concerned about his or her ability to make a living. However, the kinds of stress and the solutions available are quite different for the impoverished black teenager in the inner city than they are for the white middle-class suburban youth.

Young people living in poverty must master very basic skills—in reading, writing, and deference to authority—that may not have been successfully stressed in school and often were discouraged in their peer group. They must often deal with the prejudices of the larger society regarding color and with their own concepts about self-worth. White suburbanites, on the other hand, face a less overwhelming, but still troublesome, set of stresses. These adolescents are plagued by pressures to compete and succeed that are likely to be continuous and all-pervasive in school, at home, and in their peer group. There is a sense, too, that they must hurry and grow up, that who they are or may be is less important than what they will do and how much money they will make doing it. Their present, with its joys and heartaches, is devalued by the future to which it is mortgaged.

THE SYMPTOMS OF STRESS

The symptoms of stress may appear in any or all aspects of an adolescent's life. Sometimes they are manifested, as with adults, in physical illnesses: Asthma, arthritis, hypertension, and colitis all appear in adolescents and are all stress related. More often adolescents show their stress in their feelings and the ways they choose to cope with them and in the challenges they avoid and the behaviors that help to avoid them. Depression and suicide, alcohol and drug abuse, dropping out of school, teenage pregnancy, delinquency, accidents, and homicides are all symptoms of the distress that adolescents feel.

POVERTY AND STRESS

Although one or more symptoms of stress may occur in the life of any adolescent, all of them are far more common in adolescents from poor families—at least in urban and suburban areas in developed countries—than they are in middle-class young people. This makes sense. Poverty and the conditions it brings with it are incredibly powerful stressors.

Young people from poor families are subject to greater biological stress (from a less adequate diet and poorer prenatal care), psychological stress (there is a far higher incidence of divorce, single-parent families, and psychological problems among the poor), physical stress (child abuse is as much as eight times as common), and environmental stress (from greater overcrowding, pollution, and crime). They go to more crowded schools where they are generally taught less adequately and live in disintegrating neighborhoods where fear, bitterness, and hopelessness are as common and as hard to overcome as the poverty and crime that help to create them.

COPING POORLY WITH STRESS

Adolescents use a number of means to cope with the stress they feel. Some are creative and productive. Athletic activity, for example, is both interesting in itself and a powerful and sophisticated stress reduction technique. There are other reactions to stress that can be devastating. These include depression or, in extreme cases, suicide; producing physiological relaxation and/ or a heightened sense of well-being by chemical means; and developing a group identity through collective delinquent behavior. Although more frequent among poor teenagers, the use of these strategies is prevalent among all adolescents.

Depression in adolescents is more often a symptom than a disease, a heightening of some of the normal but painful feelings of growing up rather than a permanent condition. It is a state of mind in which one feels bad about oneself and discouraged about the future, hopeless about one's prospects and helpless to alter one's fate. Sadly, sometimes these feelings—the sense of hopelessness and helplessness—become so deep that young people attempt to kill themselves: There are currently approximately 500,000 reported suicide attempts among teenagers in the United States each year, an increase of some 300% since 1965. More than 5,000 teenagers actually do kill themselves each year. In addition, fatal accidents—some of which may be attributed to an excessive risk taking that is itself a thinly disguised form of suicide—are consistently one of the leading causes of death among adolescents.

Drugs and alcohol are ways of coping with stress, attempts to reduce anxiety and alleviate depression. Unfortunately, the attempted cure often becomes worse than the disease. Each year in the United States alone, some 4.6 million adolescents between

Rebellion against authority is one common outlet for an adolescent's feelings of frustration.

the ages of 14 and 17 experience some of the negative consequences of drinking, including arrest, involvement in an accident, and impairment of health or job performance; in addition, some 10,000 people between the ages of 16 and 24 die each year in alcohol-related incidents, including car accidents, drownings, homicides, suicides, and fires.

Although less widespread than alcohol abuse, drug abuse is every bit as destructive. Marijuana, which may, if used occasionally, have few adverse consequences, all too easily becomes a means for coping with everyday stress. What was once recreational becomes habitual and, eventually, addictive. In many cases the long-term heavy use of marijuana produces a far deeper depression than the one that occasional use was meant to alleviate. And, for some young people, the drug becomes a way of life, a kind of detour from the ordinary satisfactions and learning experiences of adolescence.

Other drugs, such as the hallucinogen phencyclidine (PCP), cocaine, and the smokable crack cocaine are far more physically destructive to the brain and more psychologically disorienting and disturbing. Although fewer young people are using PCP than 10 years ago, the incidence of cocaine use is climbing rapidly. In 1985, a National Institute on Drug Abuse survey estimated that in the United States 2.5 million 18 to 24 year olds and 400,000 14 to 17 year olds had used cocaine at least once in the 30 days before the survey. Although exact figures are not available, it is clear that since then the use of cocaine, and particularly of crack, has only increased.

Addiction, particularly to crack, is hard to avoid even after one or two experiences. To the new user, crack—which is cheap and easily available, acts with lightning speed and is incredibly exhilarating—seems a magic answer, an antidote to chronic unhappiness, a way to feel on top of things, to make the world bright with possibility. All too soon, however, crack use begins to produce serious disturbances of thought processes and to make normal activities at school or work impossible. Not long after, life changes even more, as all but the wealthiest young people must resort to criminal behavior to supply their habits. Finally, continued use brings about paranoid states that are far more frightening and disabling than the original stressors the user was trying to avoid.

• • • •

. . . .

CHAPTER 6

TECHNIQUES FOR REDUCING STRESS

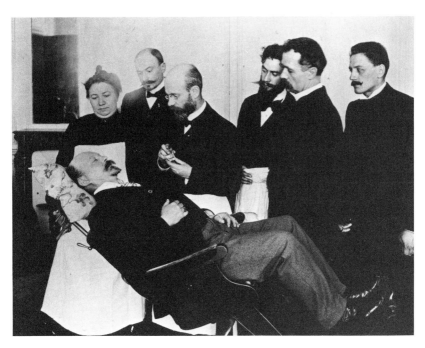

A hypnosis demonstration

Every culture has its stress reduction techniques. In India people have been using the postures of hatha-yoga and the breathing techniques of *pranayama*—meaning "breath control"—for thousands of years to promote relaxation and a sense of well-being. In ancient Athens physical exercise and relaxing baths were seen as the appropriate complement to mental exertions. Western Europeans and Americans have for centuries celebrated the psychological and physical benefits of a brisk "constitutional" walk, a quiet vacation in the mountains or by the sea, and a healthy attitude toward life. The modern approach to stress reduction includes all of these and focuses them more precisely on the host of new stresses that have developed during the modern age and on the variety of physical and psychological problems that are prevalent today.

Modern stress reduction techniques are based on four major premises:

1. It is possible for people to become aware of those factors in their lives that are primarily responsible for the stress they are experiencing.

2. The individual who wants to has the capacity to make a difference in the way he or she responds to stress.

3. Since stress—and the stress-related illnesses to which chronic stress may contribute—can be produced by habits, attitudes, emotions, relationships, and actions, changes in any or all of these can help alleviate stress and reverse the consequences of stress-related illnesses.

4. The major pathways by which stress exerts its destructive effects—including the autonomic nervous, endocrine, and immune systems—are far more amenable to the individual's conscious control than Western scientists have heretofore believed.

INVESTIGATING THE CAUSES OF STRESS

The major ingredient in any investigation of the sources of stress is honesty. In this context honesty means a willingness to look squarely at those aspects of one's life that are disturbing, those ways of thinking and being that are doing a disservice to one's health and well-being. Because most stress is the product of many years of conflict rather than the result of a single catastrophic event, these patterns are deeply ingrained. And often, it is precisely those attitudes and practices to which people are most devoted—the ones they have least wanted to question or change—that are responsible for their difficulties.

Most people are willing to be honest in this way only when the stakes are high, when they feel terribly troubled or disabled by what they are doing or badly frightened of the possible consequences of these actions. This is why so many people enter stress reduction programs only after being told that they may be developing a life-threatening illness or when they are so troubled that they cannot function normally.

A person who has decided to begin a process of honest self-appraisal has several approaches to choose from. Although these strategies may be described, and combined, in various ways, there are two general kinds: the introspective and the retrospective. The introspective depends on an intuitive knowledge of what is or has been troubling us most deeply; the retrospective depends on a process of taking an inventory of the events that have occurred.

Introspective approaches are often facilitated by conversations with a counselor, therapist, or physician, who makes use of techniques that heighten attention and bypass conscious awareness to access the hidden or unconscious parts of the mind. These include Freud's original techniques of dream analysis and "free association," in which a person lies in a comfortable position and says whatever comes to his or her mind; and more recent and focused procedures, including questioning under hypnosis, use of "guided imagery," and interpretation of drawings. These techniques may play a vital part in relieving as well as discovering the sources of stress.

Hypnosis (from *Hypnos*, the Greek god of sleep) is actually a state characterized by a combination of relaxation and increased alertness and suggestibility. This hypnotic, or "trance," state may be induced by the hypnotist's tone of voice; by repetitive stimulation (as by watching a pendulum or metronome); by a series of suggestions involving relaxation; or by stories involving confusion or mind-boggling paradoxes. All of these seem to diminish the ordinary logic and careful censorship of the conscious mind to produce both a heightened awareness and greater access to forgotten memories. When the hypnotist asks the hypnotized person questions he or she has not been able to resolve on a conscious level—such as "Why are you feeling poorly?" or "What is the major source of your stress?" the patient may, to his or her surprise, find it easy to answer the questions directly.

Guided imagery, like hypnosis, can be used to facilitate access to the unconscious and to repressed memories. A therapist who is using guided imagery may begin by asking a person to feel a physical symptom of his stress—for example, a persistent feeling of tightness in the chest. Then a dialogue begins. The therapist may ask the patient to see the tightness. "It's a knot," the patient says. "Who tied the knot?" the therapist may ask, and a mental image of the patient's boss appears; in time the boss's face may change into that of the patient's father, and early memories, of being inhibited or tied up—figuratively, or in some cases literally—may emerge.

Drawings, which psychotherapists who work with children have used as a major tool for many years, may bring similar results. Giving one's stress a visual form activates the right side of the brain, where the language of the unconscious flourishes. The symbols people use to represent their stresses provide a point of departure for the imaginative investigation of their causes, in much the same way as guided imagery. The retrospective approach depends on making an inventory of significant life changes and life events during recent months or years. Most often this involves filling out a questionnaire that is more or less loosely based on Thomas Holmes's Schedule of Recent Events. The questions raised offer an excellent survey of the factors that have produced stress and provides a method for quantifying the amount of stress as well as identifying its kind. It lacks the historical sweep and the intimate specificity of the introspective approach, but it is an excellent screening device and is easily administered to large numbers of people. In addition, such questions may trigger memories of earlier, similar stresses.

The two approaches—the introspective and the retrospective—are natural complements in diagnosing the sources of stress. In addition, both serve therapeutic functions. Knowing the source of one's stress makes it possible to begin to deal with the cause as well as the effects of it. Moreover, this knowledge is the first step in a process of reversing the feelings of helplessness and hopelessness that contribute so greatly to stress-related illness. Finally, there are neurophysiologists who believe that simply reexperiencing painful memories that have been excluded from consciousness may alter the nature of those memories by making them accessible and therefore subject to integration with other mental experiences. This process of integration in turn redefines stressful experiences by putting them in a larger context and diminishes their capacity to produce additional harm.

CHANGING ONE'S ATTITUDE TOWARD STRESS

Some attitudes and ways of dealing with the inevitable conflicts that life brings contribute to the maintenance of high levels of stress and tend to be implicated in the production of stress-related illness. Though there are many aspects to these attitudes, two general patterns emerge. These may be described as: (1) a time-driven compulsiveness and a desperate need to live up to others' expectations, coupled with a refusal to look at or meet one's own needs; and (2) a sense that one is hopeless and helpless to change either the world or one's own condition and is dependent on others for one's sense of well-being. The former corresponds roughly to the Type A personality, the latter to the "cancer-prone" personality. The former tends to be exhibited by people who are anxious and insecure, the latter by the depressed and needy.

As noted in earlier chapters, people whose lives are shaped by either of these attitudes are likely to have alterations in their biology that are destructive—excesses of sympathetic nervous system activity, depletions of the immune system, anxiety, and depression all have unhealthy effects on the body. Virtually all of the techniques that have been devised to change attitudes are designed to be antidotes to either the anxious compulsiveness or the hopelessness and helplessness or to both of them at once. By reversing these attitudes, it is believed, a person will be able to prevent the adverse emotional and physical consequences of stress and to ameliorate or reverse the illnesses to which they may have contributed.

In fact, there is already some evidence to support this. Dr. Suzanne Kobasa and her colleagues have identified a "stress-hardy" personality. These people, who deal with a great deal of apparent life stress, seem to be protected from its adverse emotional and physical consequences by their attitude toward life.

In 1985, Cleveland State University professors Boaz Kahana and Zev Harel interviewed 150 survivors of the Nazi holocaust and found that these survivors had heightened abilities to cope with life's common problems and tragedies.

According to Kobasa, this attitude is characterized by commitment, control, and challenge. Commitment entails an interest in and involvement with what is happening in one's life; control implies the sense that one can do something to influence the events that affect one's life; and challenge reflects a belief that potentially stressful change is best understood as an opportunity for creative response rather than a misfortune.

COGNITIVE THERAPIES

Cognitive (from the Latin *cognoscere*, "to know") therapies are therapies that attempt to change the way people think about themselves and their life. Such therapies may be seen as influencing the cerebrocortical aspect of stress, which in turn shapes the emotional response of the limbic-hypothalamic system.

There are many different varieties of cognitive therapy, embracing a number of different techniques. This volume touches on only a few of these techniques, including the refuting of irrational ideas, thought stopping, and assertiveness training.

Refuting irrational ideas is a technique that grows out of the work of Albert Ellis, a psychologist who in the early 1960s created what he called Rational Emotive Therapy. Ellis believed that emotional responses—and particularly such responses as anxiety, anger, and depression—were not created by the events that seemed to be their origin but by the "self-talk," the thoughts used to evaluate these events.

Ellis recognized that such self-talk was the product of psychological history, but instead of investigating that history as most therapists did, he chose to focus on ways of changing the thoughts that dictated the self-talk. He developed a method for discovering and changing stress-producing self-talk that is now used both by therapists working with clients and by those who want to work on their own.

The first step in refuting irrational ideas is discovering what those destructive, limiting, and untrue ideas or beliefs are. Though they are of many different kinds, most share certain common characteristics: The person believes that most of his or her unhappiness can be attributed to what others have done to him or her; that the person is hopelessly dependent on others; that the future is dangerous; and that unless he or she is perfect he or she cannot be satisfied. Once these beliefs have been discovered, the individual is in a position to take a look at his or her response to a stressful situation and begin to change the nature of his or her self-talk about it.

The Relaxation and Stress Reduction Workbook (see Resource section) outlines a five-step process for changing self-talk: (1) write down the facts of the event; (2) write down your self-talk about the event; (3) focus on and label your emotional response; (4) dispute and change the irrational self-talk using your understanding of the irrational ideas that have shaped your emotions; and (5) substitute alternative self-talk that reflects your understanding that your previous beliefs were irrational and that you can shape your emotions.

Thought stopping is a technique that many behavior therapists have used to treat people who are preoccupied with repetitive and irrational thoughts that interfere with their normal func-

Henri Fuseli's The Nightmare *vividly depicts some of the fearful and obsessive thoughts that are hallmarks of mental illness.*

tioning. These thoughts may be primarily phobic (from the Greek word *phobos*, meaning "flight" or "fear") as in I'm terrified of being alone in my house, or obsessive (from the Latin *obsidere*, "to beset"), as for example, Nobody in my class likes me. Generally, as is apparent from the examples, the elements of fear and obsessiveness are present together.

After taking an inventory of one's stressful thoughts and rating them in order of the discomfort they produce, one can begin the actual process of thought stopping. This involves four steps: (1) allowing oneself to dwell on one of the stressful thoughts for a period of time; (2) interrupting the stressful thought by a prerecorded command to "Stop" or with a signal from a timer; (3) calling an end to one's rumination on the obsessive or phobic thought, by shouting or saying "Stop"; and (4) substituting a positive thought for the disturbing one—for example, instead of I'm terrified of being alone in my house, one thinks, I can relax here, by myself and do whatever I want. Both refuting irrational ideas and thought stopping are active techniques that depend on the individual's conviction that he or she can, by a conscious exercise of will and rational intelligence, alter his or her cognitive and emotional response to stress. Assertiveness training assumes that the same abilities can be mobilized to help people deal with and change the interpersonal sources of stress.

Like the other techniques, assertiveness training begins with taking an inventory, in this case an inventory of the ways and situations in which one is either aggressive (accusatory, inconsiderate, etc.), passive (submissive and compliant in spite of feelings to the contrary), or assertive (standing up for oneself without being hurtful or offensive). The situations in which one is either aggressive or passive are described in specific detail, and a script is devised for changing them so that one can be assertive in them. Among the guidelines for making these changes are the following: (1) making as objective a description of the situation as possible, without blaming yourself or the other person; (2) describing your own feelings using "I" statements, not descriptions of the other person's shortcomings; and (3) making as specific a statement as possible of what your wants are.

SELF-REGULATION STRATEGIES

Techniques for self-regulation include relaxation therapies, hypnosis, biofeedback, guided imagery, and meditation. All are based on the ability of the mind to control the body and many of its functions, and all involve the mind's capacity to create antidotes to many aspects of the stress response.

Though these approaches vary considerably in their complexity and specificity, all have at least the following effects on the body's functions: They increase the predominance (in the cerebral cortex) of lower-frequency, higher-amplitude alpha waves, which indicate relaxation, over high-frequency beta waves characteristic of arousal; they decrease the dominance of the sympathetic nervous system and increase the activity of the relaxation-oriented parasympathetic nervous system; they slow respiratory and heart rate and decrease blood pressure; they decrease output of epinephrine and the stress hormones cortisone, cortisol, and thyroxine; improve the effectiveness of the immune response in its defensive and surveillance functions; increase levels of relaxation-producing neuropeptides; relax skeletal muscles; warm hands and feet; and produce a general sense of well-being.

Relaxation therapies are the simplest of the self-regulatory techniques. One of the most popular and easiest to learn, "progressive muscular relaxation," was first developed by Edmund Jacobson, an American physician, in 1929 and later modified in various ways. It involves contraction and then relaxation of all of the major voluntary muscle groups in the body, beginning with the feet and extending upward to include the legs, pelvis, stomach, back, chest, arms, neck, and head.

The practitioner may tense the muscles while breathing in and relax them while exhaling. The contraction and relaxation may be accompanied by a phrase of autosuggestion (self-hypnosis) such as "I am" (breathe in/contract muscles) "relaxed" (breathe out/relax muscles). More complex relaxation therapies, such as autogenic training, include a variety of different autosuggestions that may combine with guided imagery and deep breathing to produce physiological effects that diminish the stress response.

Biofeedback refers to the feedback of information about biological processes. It is based on the idea that people who are given information about their body's internal processes can use this information to learn to control these processes. For example, a man who is presented with continuous information about fluctuations of temperature in his hands (through a sensor attached to his finger that displays his temperature on a screen) can learn to raise or lower his own temperature. In a similar way, individuals can use information about their heart rate and brain waves to alter and control them.

Biofeedback can thus be used to diminish the stress response at a number of levels, including the cerebral cortex and the ANS. It is also a valuable tool in addressing the problems of specific stress-related illnesses. For example, an overactive sympathetic nervous system, which causes widespread constriction of arteries, seems to be an important factor in migraine headaches. If people who suffer from migraines can learn to relax the arteries in their hands by using a biofeedback device to teach them to warm their hands, they can often obtain relief from their migraines. Hypnosis and guided imagery, which have been discussed above as diagnostic techniques, are also powerful means for self-regulation. Both of these tools can be used either to obtain a generalized reduction in stress level or to improve one's confidence about dealing with stress. They can also be used to bring

Dr. Edmund Jacobson with the neurovoltmeter, which he invented in 1940 to measure tension levels. Eleven years earlier Dr. Jacobson had developed progressive muscular relaxation, one of the most widely used relaxation therapies.

about specific changes in the stress response that are of use in the treatment of illnesses.

Hypnosis can be used not only to reduce the stress that contributes to the onset of arthritis but also to diminish the pain. A variety of suggestions can be used. In one technique a patient with arthritis in her knees is asked, while under hypnosis, to imagine that she is walking into ice-cold water. Once the water, with its numbing effect, gets to her knees, the pain begins to disappear. Studies on this technique have also shown that the decrease in pain is accompanied by a decrease in the inflammation that causes the pain. Thus, hypnosis is treating the cause as well as the symptoms of the illness.

Guided imagery may be used in many of the same situations as hypnosis (indeed, there is some controversy about whether the two are not simply different ways of describing the same phenomenon). One of its most fascinating applications is its use as a means to improve the surveillance function of the immune system. This surveillance function, in which white blood cells destroy abnormal cells, is of great importance in both the prevention of and recovery from cancer.

In a typical guided imagery exercise a cancer patient might be encouraged to imagine his or her white blood cells as brave knights on white horses, attacking the sniveling, cowardly cancer cells. In fact, studies show that using guided imagery in this way (presumably its effect proceeds from the cortex to the hypothalamus to the thymus and other structures of the immune system) does increase the numbers and improve the functioning of the cells responsible for surveillance.

Meditation (derived from Latin and Greek words for "thought," "care," and "cure") is one of the most complex of the self-regulation strategies for stress reduction, and in many ways the most misunderstood. This is partly because the term covers so many different practices from so many different cultural traditions and partly because many people tend to confuse it with relaxation.

Some forms of meditation, such as the relaxation therapies (and biofeedback, hypnosis, and guided imagery), simply produce a greater feeling of calm and the physiological responses characteristic of reduced stress. These include Transcendental Meditation, which uses a simple mantra in the form of a meaningless word repeated silently for 20 minutes twice a day as a focusing device; and the Relaxation Response of the Harvard cardiologist Dr. Herbert Benson, which makes use of a variety of different sounds ("one" is frequently suggested) and prayers in a similar fashion. These techniques have repeatedly been documented as effective in reducing blood pressure, increasing the incidence of alpha brain waves, and improving practitioners' overall sense of well-being.

There are, however, many other forms of meditation that are less focused on relaxation and the physiology of stress and more concerned with changing the fundamental attitude that causes one to see events as stressful. These meditation techniques include: paying "bare attention" to the breath or the sensations in the body (Tibetan *vipassana*, or "mindfulness"); wrestling with a paradoxical saying (the Zen *koan*); whirling in a circle (the dervishes of Asia Minor); humming or bowing repeatedly (Tibetan Buddhists); or simply practicing "choiceless awareness" (J. Krishnamurti). Though the means—and the physiological responses that accompany them—vary, the goal is similar: a kind of dispassionate awareness that the meditator will bring with

Religious leader Jeddu Krishnamurti promoted a concept called choiceless awareness as a meditation technique.

him or her into all aspects of daily life, a sense of complete appreciation of every moment of life, whatever it may be like, coupled with a lack of worry about what has happened or may occur. From this perspective what seems to be stress cannot be distressing.

NUTRITIONAL APPROACHES TO STRESS MANAGEMENT

Twenty-five hundred years ago the ancient Greek physician Hippocrates told his students:

"Let food be your medicine, and medicine your food." During the last century this advice has been ever more consistently ignored. Modern society's efforts have been directed to producing more food faster and cheaper, to finding ever more attractive ways to flavor, package, and market food, and to keeping food preserved for ever longer times.

Much of what people eat is raised in soils polluted by herbicides and pesticides and degraded by overuse. Meat and poultry are contaminated by hormones, antibiotics, and other chemicals designed to make animals grow faster and larger. Vitamins and minerals and fiber and bulk are processed out of food that is then preserved only by the addition of toxic or, indeed, carcinogenic (cancer-causing) substances. Cooking is done at destructively high heats. And when it finally comes time to eat this food, people often do so hurriedly, while watching television, driving a car, or reading a newspaper. Food is no longer a source of health but a major source of stress.

The amount of information about nutrition is vast, but the conclusive evidence for the efficacy of one or another diet is scanty. Still, there are a few general principles that are useful in helping to remove the stresses diet causes and in making food once again a good medicine. Some of these have to do with attitudes toward food and the way poeple eat: Everyone should eat more slowly and spend more time at the dinner table. In addition, everyone should pay more attention to what foods are bought and how they are prepared.

The specific dietary changes include reducing the amount of fats, particularly animal fats, and processed food (the high intake of both has been implicated in chronic illnesses, including several kinds of cancer), cutting down on sugar and caffeine (which stress the endocrine and autonomic nervous systems) as well as salt (which is a significant contributor to hypertension) and artificial food flavorings and additives (some of which, including monosodium glutamate—MSG—can be toxic).

On the positive side, everyone should eat more raw food in general and more complex carbohydrates, including whole grains, which are digested more slowly than sugars and processed grains and are high in the fiber that makes digestive processes more efficient. In addition to eliminating some of the most harmful parts of the diet and introducing foods that are more healthful, these changes will also help curb obesity, which itself is a major source of psychological and physiological stress.

PHYSICAL EXERCISE

Physical exercise acts directly and indirectly to counteract the effects of the stress response. The indirect benefits include a sense of mastery and feelings of pleasure and satisfaction. The direct benefits vary according to the kind of exercise and whether or not the exercise is aerobic.

Aerobic exercises, which are activities that increase oxygen consumption, include running and jogging, swimming, bicycling, dance, and such continuous-motion sports as basketball, soccer, field hockey, and lacrosse. In general, aerobic exercise takes the tension and energy that the fight-or-flight response makes available and puts it to good use. Exercising at least 20 minutes 3 times a week decreases the levels of fats and cholesterol in the blood and improves the functioning of the heart; postexercise results include lowered heart rate and blood pressure. Moreover, aerobic exercise also increases the level of endorphins and catecholamines (chemicals that resemble epinephrine and are depleted in depressed people) in the brain. These changes contribute to a feeling of well-being, a fact confirmed by several studies on the successful use of jogging in the treatment of depression.

There are a wide variety of nonaerobic exercises ranging from bowling, baseball, and golf to less familiar exercises borrowed from other cultures, including yoga, aikido, and t'ai chi ch'uan. Though all may be emotionally relaxing to participants and provide some degree of mental and physical stimulation, some Oriental exercises offer a unique combination of physical and emotional benefits.

Yoga, for example, combines slow deep breathing with a variety of gentle stretches in a way that works directly on the autonomic nervous system to decrease dominance of the sympathetic nervous system; studies have shown that the regular practice of hatha-yoga postures can be helpful in the treatment of anxiety, depression, hypertension, asthma, diabetes, and arthritis.

Proper breathing is a part of all exercise, but breathing has also been practiced as a separate stress reduction exercise for thousands of years. Slow deep breathing, in through the nose and out through the mouth, can be extremely relaxing. Focus on counting the breaths from 1 to 10 and then backwards from 10 to 1, and you have a Zen meditation technique that also provides relaxation. For those whose stress is manifested as depression, very fast deep breathing, in and out through the nose (an ancient Tibetan technique), can be quite energizing.

MUTUAL SUPPORT GROUPS

Mutual support groups directly address the feelings of isolation and hopelessness that contribute to and compound stress. These groups consist of people who are suffering from the same illness (hypertension, colitis, etc.) or the same stressful situation (runaway teenagers, battered women, or lonely older people) or are making use of the same self-destructive responses to stress (alcohol, drugs, gambling, etc.). The very nature of the group lets participants know they are not alone. In it, members share their strategies for coping with the stresses that contribute to their illnesses or social problems and the stresses that these in turn create. Moreover, the presence of people who have successfully dealt with their problems provides an example and inspiration for all members.

Though many different kinds of mutual support groups have been helpful, it is worth singling out Alcoholics Anonymous (AA) and the other "12-step" groups that have been modeled after it. These leaderless groups, which include Narcotics Anonymous (NA), Gamblers Anonymous (GA), and Overeaters Anonymous (OA), have millions of members and charge no fees. They are called 12-step groups because each is based on a program that consists of 12 therapeutic steps. The first step in these programs requires participants to admit that they are "powerless" in the face of their addiction—whether to alcohol or drugs or food. Later they are asked to turn their healing over to "a higher power." It is interesting to note that these successful, popular programs combine the ordinary stress reduction procedures of personal honesty, confidence building, attitude changing, and mutual support with a perspective that puts human life into a larger spiritual context.

•   •   •   •

CHAPTER 7
. . . .
STRESS MANAGEMENT PROGRAMS

A participant in a seniors' growth-awareness project.

Twenty years ago stress management programs were all but unknown. Today they are everywhere—in hospitals and private physicians' offices, in schools and, most often, at the work site. They are there for several reasons. The initial stimulus was society's growing awareness in the late 1960s and early 1970s of the role of stress in producing and maintaining the vast majority of chronic illnesses. To this was added a new perspective on health care.

This "wellness approach" or "wellness medicine" emphasized the maintenance of wellness in addition to the treatment of illness. From this point of view, not being ill and being well were two different categories. Wellness implied a positive state—vitality, happiness, and creativity, not just the absence of disease. And, proponents added, a high degree of wellness could be achieved even in the presence of chronic illness.

This new interest in wellness dovetailed nicely with the fitness boom—the greatly expanded interest in exercise and proper diet—of the early 1970s, with the importation of a variety of meditation techniques from the East to the West, and with a revival of interest in self-help and mutual help as health care strategies.

One result of the confluence of these forces was the creation of a holistic (from *holos*, the Greek word for "whole"), or wholistic, approach to medicine. This strategy emphasized the treatment of the whole person in his or her total environment, patient responsibility, and the integration of such alternative approaches as meditation and acupuncture with conventional Western medicine. Another result was the development of educationally oriented stress management programs. Increasingly it seemed—to both providers and recipients of health care—that people could take more responsibility for managing their stress and maintaining their own health and that many of the necessary skills could be easily transferred from experts to everybody.

In time, this mixture of new understanding, attitude, and technique was catalyzed by the realization that stress-related illnesses were costing an enormous amount of money: A recent U.S. government study estimates that stress-related disorders are costing U.S. industry "as much as $150 billion a year due to the decreased productivity resulting from diminished functionability, disability, and absenteeism." By the mid-1980s it had become clear to many health care providers and most corporations that programs to manage stress were an economic necessity as well as a health benefit.

From the beginning, stress management programs have tended to fall into three categories, each reflecting the concerns of those who created the programs: programs run by physicians and other health care providers for patients with diagnosed illnesses; wellness-based programs run by groups of health care providers or hospitals; and programs run by employers and based at the work site, and, in the case of young people, at school. Each of these kinds of programs shares common assumptions about the destructive consequences of stress and the possibility of relieving it, or, indeed, converting it into a positive force, by changing one's attitudes and habits.

STRESS PROGRAMS FOR CHRONIC CONDITIONS

In the early 1970s, a number of physicians began to reevaluate the way they treated people with such chronic physical illnesses as hypertension, arthritis, cancer, diabetes, and chronic musculoskeletal pain. During their years in practice, they had come to see the limitations of conventional surgical and pharmacological therapies; now, as they read the new reports on the effects of stress on the body, on the use of biofeedback and meditation to lower blood pressure and treat migraine headaches and asthma, they began to reformulate their approach.

Specialists in the treatment of cancer and heart disease, in surgery, pediatrics, and family practice, consulted with psychiatrists to learn more about the effects of emotional and cognitive processes on the body; experts in physiology, such as Dr. Herbert Benson, studied the effects of meditation on blood pressure and heart rate and experimented with teaching relaxation techniques to nonmeditators. In time, some of these men and women would create comprehensive stress management programs designed to meet the needs of the specific group of patients they treated.

At Beth Israel Hospital in Boston, Benson and his co-workers set up the Behavioral Medicine Unit, which initially focused on psychological aspects of cardiovascular disease and the therapeutic use of self-regulation strategies. In Fort Worth, Texas, Dr. Carl Simonton, a specialist in radiation oncology (the use of radiation to treat cancer) and his wife, Stephanie Matthews-Simonton, established the Cancer Counseling and Rehabilitation Center, a program that combined stress management techniques with such conventional cancer treatments as radiation therapy and chemotherapy. The Simontons combined guided imagery with individual and family counseling and mutual help groups as a means of stimulating the immune system of cancer patients

This BETAR (Bio Energetics Training Resource) surrounds its occupant with music, which relaxes the occupant and stimulates pleasant feelings.

and thus improving their chances of dealing successfully with their illness. Meanwhile, in La Crosse, Wisconsin, Dr. C. Norman Shealy, a neurosurgeon who founded the American Holistic Medical Association, created a center for the control of chronic pain.

Shealy's approach is particularly interesting because it has evolved over time, has been widely emulated, and makes use of a wide variety of techniques for stress management. By the late 1960s, Shealy was becoming disillusioned with his efforts as a neurosurgeon. The operations he did were often helpful to people who had suffered acute, life-threatening trauma to the head. But much of his practice consisted of people with chronic back pain. Surgery often did not help them; pain-relieving drugs created side effects and did not ultimately relieve that much pain. Even newer surgical and electrical procedures worked only a small percentage of the time.

When Shealy began to look for reasons why so few people responded even to the best treatment, he discovered that a variety of psychological factors, including his patients' attitudes and their general level of stress, were interfering with their recovery. He developed an intensive residential program to address these factors. Each year as many as 200 people with chronic pain would spend 2 to 4 weeks participating in a comprehensive therapy and education program that included exercise, biofeedback, psychotherapy, and relaxation and guided imagery techniques, as well as physical therapy, electrical stimulation of the nerves, and acupuncture.

By the time Shealy moved his Pain and Health Rehabilitation Center to Springfield, Missouri, in the mid-1980s, he had expanded its scope to include patients with a variety of chronic health problems. Over the years he had learned that his holistic approach to stress management could be useful to people with asthma, arthritis, hypertension, and cancer as well as to those with chronic pain. Interestingly, many other programs that began to work with one illness have enlarged their focus to include others. Similarly, programs that began with one or two stress management techniques have expanded to include many more.

Medical workers in China learn acupuncture skills. This ancient Chinese technique has become a popular approach to minimizing stress in Western society as well.

Of all stress management programs, the ones that have helped people with chronic illness have been most successful—for both immediate relief of symptoms and long-term gains. For example, a study done of Shealy's pain relief program and published in a volume entitled *Mind, Body & Health*, revealed that 72% of the patients who completed the program maintained their improvement or had even less pain a year later. This is not surprising. Programs—some of them quite expensive—that focus on chronic illness provide a high ratio of skilled staff to patients, a great deal of one-to-one attention, and a considerable amount of mutual support. Perhaps most important, the people who enter these programs are highly motivated both by their present suffering and by the expectation that if they do not do something different they will only get worse.

WELLNESS PROGRAMS

In 1975, John Travis, a physician with a strong interest in public health, founded the Wellness Resource Center in Mill Valley, California. Wellness, he said, was "a state of being, an attitude, an ongoing process . . . not simply the absence of illness." Lack of wellness was manifested by those who felt "bored, tense, anxious, or generally depressed with their lives." These people did not have a disease, but they were not well either.

They did not, Travis believed, need treatment, but they did need teaching to help them to feel as well as they could. The approach he developed was, accordingly, an educational one, using workbooks, classes, dialogues, and audiovisual materials.

Travis created a 5-part program that included the Wellness Evaluation, a 300-question self-assessment tool that focused on how one's way of life (including smoking, eating, drinking, and working habits) and attitude related to health; on "body awareness" techniques, including biofeedback and massage, which were designed to help participants feel and dissolve the tenseness that stress produced; on dietary counseling; on psychological counseling designed to help people break stress-producing habits; and on a group experience, similar to assertiveness training, that Travis called "communicating your needs."

Travis's program helped inspire the creation of the Swedish Wellness Program at the Swedish Medical Center in Engelwood, Colorado, and it in turn became a model for wellness programs in and outside of hospitals. Many hundreds of these programs have started since 1975. Some of them are offered by residential health spas, like Arizona's Canyon Ranch, where visitors may come for a week of stress management training and conditioning; others, like the Swedish Wellness Program, are available locally, in hospitals, physicians' offices, and health clubs.

Though the specific techniques vary widely, Travis's general emphasis persists: These are educational programs, combining self-awareness with relaxation, body awareness, self-regulation, and attitude change; new information about the mind and body, dietary changes and life-style choices are presented in a classroom format; and individual counseling and group sessions are used to promote self-examination and mutual support.

In general, these wellness programs are used by people who may be hurried and harrassed but do have a certain amount of leisure time; in many cases, they also have disposable income available to them. These are people who fit Travis's description of the tense, anxious, and depressed, rather than those suffering from serious psychological or physical problems. They want to change the attitudes that make them view challenging situations as stressful and to alter the self-destructive, habitual behavior—smoking, drinking, overeating—that they use to cope with stress. They are, in short, people who have satisfied many of their basic material wants but are looking for a less driven, more fulfilling, healthy, stress-free, creative life.

One study of those involved with wellness programs, also published in *Advances: The Journal for Mind-Body Health*, showed that those who attended 10 sessions of combined cognitive and relaxation training at a university stress clinic experienced an average increase in well-being of 67%. The educational approach suits those who have decided they can feel better and want to take charge of the process. The gains in well-being they make with relaxation techniques or assertiveness training provide satisfaction and reinforce the efforts they are prepared to make on their own.

WORK-SITE STRESS MANAGEMENT PROGRAMS

For most adults, work is a vitally important part of life, a source not only of income but also of identity. It indicates something about who a person is and provides a definition of how that person fits into society. It is where most adults spend at least seven hours a day, five days a week. It offers satisfaction and challenges. Work also presents most people with a wide range of stresses.

In 1975, there were few, if any, stress management programs at work sites. Today, according to a study done for the U.S. Department of Health and Human Services and published in *Advances*, two-thirds of all work sites in the United States have some kind of health promotion activity (including programs to assess health risks, stop smoking, and prevent back injuries), and more than one-half of these include stress management programs.

The motivation for this extraordinary change is, as was noted earlier, largely economic. In 1988, for example, the bill for national health care in the United States was estimated at $511 billion. Private corporations paid between 40% and 43% of this figure (which does not include the $150 billion in lost productivity). And each year both the total amount spent on medical care and the corporations' share of this bill is increasing. Moreover, the cost of insurance claims for stress-related illnesses seems to be escalating even more quickly: Stress-related claims in California increased 434% between 1982 and 1986.

Though the motivation is primarily economic, the benefits of work site stress management programs accrue to everyone. An early study of a program at Equitable Life Assurance revealed that three months after the program ended, participants had "fewer visits to the health center, decreases in stress symptoms, increases in work satisfaction, and decreases in symptom interference in work." These benefits to workers are, inevitably, matched by the benefits to the corporations. In another study, a single stress management program that was implemented in three different settings—a medium-sized hospital, a trucking company, and a small hospital—produced great savings: Accident-related losses declined from an average of $24,199 a month over the 2 years prior to the intervention to $2,577 a month over the 11 months following the intervention program.

The techniques used in work site programs are for the most part the same as those used in chronic illness and wellness programs—stress surveys, relaxation therapies, biofeedback, and assertiveness training are common. The format—a combination of classes, discussion and support groups, and one-to-one counseling—is also similar. There are, however, some important differences in emphasis that are dictated by the corporate setting and a focus on stress on the job. For example, time management seminars are a frequent ingredient in these stress programs, as are classes that focus on issues related to such on-the-job problems as relationships between supervisors and subordinates and accident prevention. Also, some programs that focus on the problems of executives are particularly concerned with the health consequences of Type A behavior.

As the experience corporations have with stress management programs has increased, certain problems have become apparent and some solutions found. Max Heirich, who helped develop and evaluate stress management programs for General Motors, lists the following lessons:

1. One-on-one outreach to workers and follow-up after the program is over are crucial to effectiveness.

2. Though some employees make good use of classes, many more are helped by individually designed, guided self-help programs.

3. Social support, from fellow workers who act as "buddies," as well as from professional counselors, is essential for maximum benefit.

4. Programs must allow people to take simple, manageable steps in decreasing stress, rather than insist on sudden, major changes.

5. Employees must be given incentives, such as time off from work to attend the program, to ensure maximum participation.

6. Finally, programs must be acceptable to labor as well as management. This means that stress reduction must not be seen as an alternative to reducing stress-producing conditions on the job but as part of an overall program designed to make the individual more healthy and the work site less stressful.

STRESS MANAGEMENT PROGRAMS FOR
ADOLESCENTS

Stress management programs for adolescents tend to resemble those developed for adults, both in the kinds of techniques used and in the focus and location of the programs. For the most part, too, there is the same rough division into programs for young people with chronic illness, wellness programs, and work site (in this case, school) programs. There are, in addition, a few programs that have dealt with the problems—and used the strengths—of adolescents in particularly interesting and creative ways.

Some comprehensive stress management programs have been developed for young people with such chronic illnesses as asthma and diabetes, but the most interesting and innovative programs to date have been designed for adolescents with emotional, behavioral, and drug- and alcohol-related problems. These agendas, both in and outside of hospitals, may combine residential treatment and individual, family, and group psychotherapy with a variety of stress management techniques. Their power in managing stress and changing the behavior that results from it, and ultimately increases it, lies in their ability to create a new world, a minisociety in which young people can live. In this new world they learn to live according to the values that are part of a stress managment program—self-awareness and self-regulation, assertiveness and mutual support, attention to physical well-being, a healthy diet, and a drug- and alcohol-free way of life.

One such program, for drug addicts, was created by the Happy Healthy Holy Organization, a yoga group in Arizona. During their stay, former addicts live a highly disciplined yogic life. They rise early in the morning, do hours of hatha-yoga postures and yogic breathing techniques, and learn a variety of relaxation and meditation techniques. They follow a caffeine-free and low-sugar vegetarian diet and participate in individual and group counseling sessions. They do useful work on the grounds and in the kitchen and participate fully in the life of their residential community.

Across the country, in an inner city mental hospital in Washington, D.C., a comprehensive program for adolescents with severe psychiatric problems was developed that, instead of using

Group therapy has proven to be a successful strategy for drug users trying to overcome their addictions.

tranquilizers and antidepressants to help patients cope with their high level of stress, taught them a variety of stress management techniques, including several relaxation therapies. Excess sugar, caffeine, fats, and food additives were removed from the hospital diet. A variety of different physical exercises, including jogging and yoga to reduce stress, were taught, in addition to meditation and relaxation techniques, as alternatives to drugs as a way to "get high."

A kung fu master was also brought in to teach twice a week. This intensive program of kung fu gave the young people, many of whom had been involved in violent crime and heavy drug abuse, a constructive outlet for their aggression as well as a sense of self-mastery and self-confidence; interestingly, it seemed to contribute significantly to lowering the incidence of violence on the ward.

Finally, a comprehensive program was developed to help these young people deal with the stresses that they would face when they returned home. In addition to remedial schooling and to group and family counseling that would continue after they left the hospital, a program of job apprenticeships was supplied within the hospital. This gave the young people an experience of working and taught them some of the skills they would need to use in dealing with employers, co-workers, and job situations "on the outside." It also provided them with the self-respect that came from being not just a patient but a useful worker—and with some spending money.

Though nonresidential stress management programs are less comprehensive, some of them also offer excellent examples of thoughtful stress management techniques tailored to the needs of adolescents. One such example is provided by wellness centers and psychotherapists in private practice who use stress reduction techniques as an integral part of family therapy. This strategy provides the family, which is often in the throes of conflict centering around the adolescent's separation, with an activity that brings them together as a unit, without implying that they need be confined by one another. It helps each member to reduce his or her own stress and simultaneously respects each person's independence and autonomy. Thus, the stress management program, with its balance of respectful togetherness and independence, can offer a model for resolving this crisis of separation in the development of both the adolescent and his or her family and also offer tools to make it go more smoothly.

Another example also relates to the adolescent's need to define him- or herself as a person separate from his or her parents. In most tribal and traditional societies, young people must constitute themselves as a separate and distinct group and pass through a series of challenges and ordeals before they can become adult members of their tribe, clan, or society. In modern Western nations, teenagers are largely left to improvise such rites of passage on their own. Without the help of older and wiser adults many of them tend to create cliques and gangs, in-groups and out-groups, to engage in the aimless or dangerous risk taking of fast cars, drugs, alcohol, meaningless sex, and premature childbearing. Some programs, such as Outward Bound and VisionQuest, provide creative and thoughtful alternatives.

In these programs young people are given the opportunity to experience their own courage and to find a peacefulness in their own nature and in the natural world. They brave dangers—of rock climbing or rappeling down the side of a cliff—that are carefully calibrated by adult leaders to make them stronger and more confident but not to debilitate them. They learn to be by themselves, in the woods or on a mountain, and to experience self-reliance. They spend time living together as a group, learning to work together and to work out their disagreements.

Feeling stronger, more confident, and more adult, they are able to put the stresses of home and school and peers in perspective, to see themselves as passing through, rather than trapped by, adolescence.

GETTING STARTED

Although the task of wrestling with self-image and sense of direction may be most intense during adolescence, no one is ever free from emotional concerns. The management of stress is a

Every person is, to some extent, responsible for his or her health and well-being.

lifetime project. As obvious as it may sound, the most important steps in designing a stress management program are deciding to do it and deciding the means, knowing deep inside that it will be done. Some people anticipate the need for this change, but most are forced by some crisis, when it becomes obvious that everything they have tried previously—job or school changes, new friends, or even cigarettes, alcohol, or other drugs—are not working. People who have acknowledged this and have decided to do something about it can choose a program best suited for them. This book has described changes in attitude and thought processes, awareness training, self-regulation strategies, physical exercise, nutrition, and other specific programs. These may be adjusted according to each person's particular needs and interests and combined in a variety of ways. Those who approach these strategies with a confident and hopeful attitude are almost always able to reduce their stress levels and thus emerge with renewed energy to lead a healthier and happier life.

•　　　•　　　•　　　•

APPENDIX:
FOR MORE INFORMATION

The following is a list of organizations that can provide further information on stress management and stress-related diseases.

GENERAL

American Institute of Stress
124 Park Avenue
Yonkers, NY 10703
(914) 963-1200

International Stress and Tension
 Control Association
Institute of Stress Management
U.S. International University
10455 Pomerado Road
San Diego, CA 92131
(619) 693-4669

Shealy Institute for Comprehensive
 Health Care
1328 East Evergreen Street
Springfield, MO 65803
(417) 865-5940

CANCER

American Cancer Society
90 Park Avenue
New York, NY 10016
(212) 599-8200

National Cancer Institute
National Institutes of Health
9000 Rockville Pike, Building 31,
 Room 10A18

Bethesda, MD 20892
(301) 496-5583
(800) 4-CANCER

National Cancer Institute of Canada
401-77 Bloor Street West
Toronto, Ontario M5S 2V7
Canada
(416) 961-7223

DIABETES

American Diabetes Association
660 Duke Street
Alexandria, VA 22314
Hot Line: (800) ADA-DISC
(703) 549-1500

Canadian Diabetes Association
78 Bond Street
Toronto, Ontario M5B 2J8
Canada
(416) 362-4440

Juvenile Diabetes Foundation
 International
432 Park Avenue South
New York, NY 10016
Hot Line: (800) 223-1138
(212) 889-7575

HEART DISEASE

American Heart Association
7320 Greenville Avenue
Dallas, TX 75231
(214) 373-6300

Canadian Heart Foundation
160 George Street
Suite 200
Ottawa, Ontario K1N 9M2
Canada
(613) 237-4361

National Heart, Lung, and Blood
Institute
National Institutes of Health
9000 Rockville Pike, Building 31,
Room 4A21
Bethesda, MD 20892
(301) 496-4236

RESEARCH CENTERS

Center for Stress Anxiety and
Disorders
State University of New York at
Albany
1535 Western Avenue
Albany, NY 12203
(518) 456-4127

Stress Physiology Laboratory
University of Nebraska
Lincoln, NE 68588
(402) 472-1161

Yale Behavioral Medicine Clinic
Yale University
25 Park Street
Hartford, CT 06519
(203) 785-2112

PICTURE CREDITS

FURTHER READING

GENERAL

Alexander, Franz. *Psychosomatic Medicine: Its Principles and Applications.* New York: Norton, 1987.

Appley, Mortimer H., and Richard A. Trumbull. *Dynamics of Stress: Physiological, Psychological, and Social Perspectives.* New York: Plenum, 1986.

Chandler, Louis A. *Children Under Stress: Understanding Emotional Adjustment Reactions.* 2nd ed. Springfield, IL: Thomas, 1985.

Cohen, Daniel, and Susan Cohen. *Teenage Stress: Understanding the Tensions You Feel at Home, at School, and Among Your Friends.* New York: Evans, 1984.

Cooper, C. L., and R. Payne. *Causes, Coping, and Consequences of Stress at Work.* New York: Wiley, 1988.

Engel, George. "A Life Setting Conducive to the Giving-up Given-in Complex." *Bulletin of Menninger Clinic* 32 (1968): 355–65.

Engel, George, and Arthur Schmale. "The Giving-up Given-in Complex." *Archives of General Psychiatry* 17 (1967): 135–45.

Gray, Jeffrey A. *The Psychology of Fear and Stress.* 2nd ed. New York: Cambridge University Press, 1988.

Hendin, Herbert, and Ann P. Haas. *Wounds of War: The Psychological Aftermath of Combat in Vietnam.* New York: Basic Books, 1984.

Hobfoll, Stevan E. *The Ecology of Stress.* New York: Hemisphere, 1988.

McLellan, Tom, and Alicia Bragg. *Escape from Anxiety and Stress.* New York: Chelsea House, 1986.

Markides, Kyriakos S., and Cary L. Cooper. *Aging, Stress, and Health.* New York: Wiley, 1989.

Orlandi, Mario, et al. *Encyclopedia of Health: Stress and Mental Health.* New York: Facts on File, 1988.

Selye, Hans. *The Stress of Life*. 2nd ed. New York: McGraw-Hill, 1978.

Shaffer, Martin. *Life After Stress*. New York: Plenum, 1982.

STRESS-RELATED ILLNESS

Bammer, Kurt, and Benjamin H. Newberry. *Stress and Cancer*. Lewiston, NY: Hogrefe International, 1981.

Beamish, R. E., et al. *Stress and Heart Disease*. Norwell, MA: Kluwer, 1985.

Cooper, C. L. *Psychological Stress and Cancer*. New York: Wiley, 1985.

Dodge, David L., and Walter T. Martin. *Social Stress and Chronic Illness: Mortality Patterns in Industrial Society*. Notre Dame, IN: University of Notre Dame Press, 1970.

Dotevall, Gerhard. *Stress and Common Gastrointestinal Disorders: A Comprehensive Approach*. New York: Praeger, 1985.

Friedman, Meyer, and Ray H. Rosenman. *Type A Behavior and Your Heart*. New York: Knopf, 1974.

Lynch, James J. *Language of the Heart: The Body's Response to Human Dialogue*. New York: Basic Books, 1985.

Wheatley, David. *Stress and the Heart*. 2nd ed. New York: Raven Press, 1981.

Zales, Michael R. *Stress in Health and Disease*. New York: Brunner-Mazel, 1985.

STRESS MANAGEMENT

Asterita, Mary F. *Physical Exercise, Nutrition, and Stress*. New York: Praeger, 1985.

Berger, Bonnie G., and Bradley D. Hatfield. *Exercise and Stress*. New York: AMS Press, 1987.

McKay, Matthew, et al. *Thoughts and Feelings: The Art of Cognitive Stress Intervention*. Oakland, CA: New Harbinger, 1981.

Meichenbaum, David, and Matt E. Jarenko. *Stress Reduction and Prevention*. New York: Plenum, 1983.

Youngs, Bettie B. *A Stress Management Guide for Young People*. Del Mar, CA: Bilicki, 1986.

GLOSSARY

adrenal cortex the outer portion of the adrenal glands; produces aldosterone, cortisol, and other hormones that control metabolic functions

adrenal medulla the inner portion of the adrenal glands; produces adrenaline and noradrenaline, hormones that help the body prepare for fight-or-flight response

adrenaline epinephrine; a hormone that is produced in the adrenal medulla and works in conjunction with noradrenaline; causes blood vessel constriction, increased heart and metabolic rates, and other actions that provide the body with extra energy in emergency situations

biofeedback the conscious monitoring of information about usually unconscious bodily processes, such as heart rate and blood pressure; a method by which patients learn to exert some control over these internal processes: Learning to relax the nervous system, for example, may help to diminish the stress response and resulting stress-related illnesses

brain organ composed of gray nerve tissue enclosed in the skull; interprets sensory impulses, coordinates and controls bodily functioning, and acts as the center of emotion and thought

cerebral cortex six layers of gray matter that form the upper and outer portion of the brain; responsible for higher mental functions, visceral functions, behavioral reactions, general movement, perception, and abstract thinking

diencephalon section of the brain that transmits emotional and sensory messages between the spinal cord and lower part of the brain and the cerebral cortex; contains the thalamus and the hypothalamus

endocrine system the system of glands located throughout the body that produce hormones and secrete them directly into the bloodstream; plays a key role in growth, reproduction, metabolism, and immune system responses

endorphin a neuropeptide that functions as an analgesic to alleviate the symptoms of stress

feedback loop the exchange of input and output between different but interrelated systems; a stabilizing process that works to maintain balance, enabling systems to exert a modifying influence over other systems

fight or flight the body's automatic response to an emergency situation; characterized by quickness of breath, increased heart and metabolic rates, and higher blood pressure; activated by the nervous system and the endocrine system to provide the body with added energy to either combat or flee from danger

general adaption syndrome (GAS) the body's reaction to long-term exposure to stress

guided imagery the use of mental images to induce relaxation or help combat a physical ailment; often used to alleviate stress and stress-related illness; considered by some to be useful as a form of hypnosis

holistic relating to or concerned with the theory that views the universe, including living organisms, as consisting of interacting wholes and complete systems rather than separate parts; by extension, holistic physicians treat the mind and the body as one system and encourage each patient to take responsibility for his or her physical health and mental well-being

homeostasis a state of equilibrium between different but interrelated functions or elements

hormone a product of the endocrine system that circulates freely throughout the bloodstream, controlling and regulating other glands and organs by chemical stimulation

hypertension persistently high blood pressure; sometimes caused by excessive aldosterone secretion

hypothalamus the section of the brain that controls the pituitary gland; regulates survival processes, such as the autonomic nervous system, reproduction, nourishment, and self-defense, by initiating the appropriate physical response through nerve impulses and chemical messengers

immune system the body's mechanism for combating viruses, bacteria, and other outside threats; composed of various types of white blood cells, including phagocytes, which consume bacteria, and lymphocytes, which produce antibodies

limbic system a group of brain structures concerned with autonomic functions and certain aspects of emotions and behavior

lymphatic system the spleen, the thymus gland, and the collection of nodes, ducts, vessels, and tissues that collectively enhance immunity by removing foreign substance from the blood and lymph, combating disease, maintaining fluid balance, and absorbing fats

meditation a technique used to bring about a relaxed state somewhat similar to that produced in hypnosis, but without rendering the subject open to suggestion; often practiced to improve mental functioning and reduce stress

milieu intérieur Claude Bernard's term for the blood and lymph that bathe the cells of the body

nervous system the organic system that, in conjunction with the endocrine system, is responsible for the adjustments and reactions of an organism to internal and environmental conditions; the central nervous system (CNS) consists of the brain and spinal cord; the peripheral nervous system registers physical sensations, such as temperature and pain; the autonomic nervous system (ANS) is divided into two parts: the sympathetic nervous system (SNS), which mobilizes outgoing energy and governs the body's reactions to arousal and external stimuli, and the parasympathetic nervous system (PNS), which maintains such internal bodily processes as energy storage, relaxation, and nourishment

neuropeptide system the system of amino acids found in the gastrointestinal tract and nervous system that transmits information among the nervous, limbic, endocrine, and immune systems; affects the emotional and biological manifestations of behavior and mood

neurophysiology the scientific study of the nervous system

noradrenaline norepinephrine; a hormone that is produced in the adrenal medulla and works in conjunction with adrenaline; causes increased blood pressure and breathing rate, as well as other reactions that provide the body with extra energy in emergency situations

ozone a form of oxygen in the upper atmosphere that protects the earth from harmful ultraviolet rays; also appears as a hazardous substance in the lower atmosphere, where it is a major component of smog

pituitary gland the "master gland"; a small gland located in the brain, attached to the hypothalamus and composed of an anterior and posterior lobe; controls the thyroid, adrenal, and sex glands; secretes several hormones

progressive muscular relaxation a relaxation technique involving contraction and then relaxation of muscles

psychoneuroimmunology the scientific study of the immune system and its interaction with the central and autonomic nervous systems and the endocrine system

psychosomatic pertaining to or caused by a combination of physiological and psychological factors

rational emotive therapy (RET) therapy emphasizing rationality and self-sufficiency over emotionalism and self-indulgence

receptor an extremely sensitive protein molecule attached to a target cell; responds to various chemical stimuli, such as hormones or neuropeptides, by triggering its target cell to react

relaxation therapy self-regulation techniques used to induce and maintain wellness and relaxation; therapies include hypnosis, biofeedback, guided imagery, and meditation

subcortex cerebral medulla; the part of the brain that lies beneath the cerebral cortex and is continuous with the spinal cord; contains nerve cells that regulate many of the body's basic processes, such as heart and breathing rates

thalamus that part of the brain containing groups of nuclei that transmit sensory impulses, such as the perception of pain, to the cerebral cortex

thymus glandular structure in the chest where T cells mature; an essential part of the immune system

ulcer open sore caused by a break in the mucous membrane or the skin

vagus nerves two nerves extending from the skull and branching into the throat, lungs, heart, stomach, bladder, intestines, and gonads; the vagus nerves channel 80% of the parasympathetic nervous system fibers

INDEX

James S. Gordon, M.D., a graduate of Harvard Medical School, practices holistic medicine in Washington, D.C., and teaches in the departments of psychiatry and community and family medicine at the Georgetown University School of Medicine. For ten years Dr. Gordon was a research psychiatrist at the National Institute of Mental Health, where he was particularly concerned with the development of innovative mental health services for adolescents and their families. He was director of the Special Study on Alternative Services for President Carter's Commission on Mental Health (1978–79). For six years, he was on the Board of Trustees of the American Holistic Medical Association. He has also served as chief of the adolescent service of St. Elizabeth's Hospital in Washington, D.C. Dr. Gordon is the author of more than 100 articles and author or editor of seven previous books, including the award-winning *Health for the Whole Person: The Complete Guide to Holistic Medicine, New Directions in Medicine,* and *The Healing Partnership.*

Solomon H. Snyder, M.D., is Distinguished Service Professor of Neuroscience, Pharmacology, and Psychiatry and director of the Department of Neuroscience at the Johns Hopkins University School of Medicine. He has served as president of the Society for Neuroscience and in 1978 received the Albert Lasker Award in Medical Research for his discovery of opiate receptors in the brain. Dr. Snyder is a member of the National Academy of Sciences and a Fellow of the American Academy of Arts and Sciences. He is the author of *Drugs and the Brain, Uses of Marijuana, Madness and the Brain, The Troubled Mind,* and *Biological Aspects of Mental Disorder.* He is also the general editor of Chelsea House's ENCYCLOPEDIA OF PSYCHOACTIVE DRUGS.

C. Everett Koop, M.D., Sc.D., is former Surgeon General, Deputy Assistant Secretary for Health, and Director of the Office of International Health of the U.S. Public Health Service. A pediatric surgeon with an international reputation, he was previously surgeon-in-chief of Children's Hospital of Philadelphia and professor of pediatric surgery and pediatrics at the University of Pennsylvania. Dr. Koop is the author of more than 175 articles and books on the practice of medicine. He has served as surgery editor of the *Journal of Clinical Pediatrics* and editor-in-chief of the *Journal of Pediatric Surgery,* Dr. Koop has received nine honorary degrees and numerous other awards, including the Denis Brown Gold Medal of the British Association of Paediatric Surgeons, the William E. Ladd Gold Medal of the American Academy of Pediatrics, and the Copernicus Medal of the Surgical Society of Poland. He is a Chevalier of the French Legion of Honor and a member of the Royal College of Surgeons, London.